CONTENTS

EQUALITY AND INEQUALITY UNDER SOCIALISM
POLAND AND HUNGARY COMPARED

Editors
Tamás Kolosi and Edmund Wnuk-Lipiński

SAGE Studies in International Sociology 29
sponsored by the International Sociological Association/ISA

SAGE Publications Ltd
28 Banner Street
London EC1Y 8QE

SAGE Publications Inc
275 South Beverly Drive
Beverly Hills, California 90212

SAGE Publications India Pvt Ltd
C-236 Defence Colony
New Delhi 110 024

British Library Cataloguing in Publication Data

Equality and inequality under socialism. — (Sage studies in international sociology; v.29)
1. Equality 2. Social policy
I. Kolosi, Tamás II. Wnuk-Lipiński, Edmund
305 HM146

ISBN 0-8039-9758-2

Library of Congress Catalog Card Number 83-050240

Printed by J. W. Arrowsmith Ltd., Bristol, UK.

PREFACE

The idea of a Hungarian-Polish comparative volume emerged in the course of work on the multinational research project undertaken by the Academies of Sciences of the following European socialist countries: Bulgaria, Czechoslovakia, GDR, Hungary, Poland, Romania and the USSR.

Initially, the prime concern of the sociologists involved was to find out whether there was any convergence taking place between manual and non-manual workers. Our colleagues from the Soviet Union (V.V. Kolbanovsky) and from the GDR (M. Lötsch) jointly elaborated the conception and programme of the comparative research project, under the auspices of the XVI Problem Commission chaired by W. Wesołowski from the Polish Academy of Sciences. The working out of research methodology took about two years. Later the unified methodological approach and questionnaires were administered in all participating countries. Hungary and Poland were represented by the authors of this book.

During these discussions we came to the conclusion that it would be useful to pay attention to the processes of differentiation as well as the processes of convergence. The general aim of the Project was defined as follows: the investigation should produce indices representing the 'distance' between four groups of industrial employees (unskilled workers, skilled workers, white-collar workers and professionals) in the participating countries, and should take into account various aspects of this phenomenon.

In the spring and summer of 1979, sociologists from the participating countries carried out research in their home countries. Data processing was completed in 1980 by the Institute of Philosophy and Sociology of the Czechoslovak Academy of Sciences, and data for this volume were processed in Hungary and Poland.

In 1979, prior to the fieldwork, Hungarian and Polish sociologists (Ferenc Kovács, Tamás Kolosi and György Akszentievics (Hungary) and Lidia Beskid, Maria Jarosińska and Edmund Wnuk-Lipiński (Poland)) agreed that, while participating in the multinational research, they would also carry out bilateral studies. This was because they anticipated a considerable similarity in the development of Polish and Hungarian industry and expected to find many common features and problems in the history of both countries. However, the reason for the Hungarian-Polish comparison was not a general, comparative exercise, but rather focused on discovering to what extent inequalities among industrial workers were similar. An attempt was made to identify and describe equalities and inequalities in a broader context, and we formed the opinion that such an approach would give us a new view of stratification in its various social dimensions.

Mention has to be made of Poland's specific circumstances. In 1980 Poland faced her most difficult crisis of the postwar period. This crisis embraced all spheres of social and political life and entailed profound transformations of economic policy. This new situation is not discussed in this volume as it is *in statu nascendi.* On the other hand, it should be noted that all Polish data were collected a year before the crisis. They may therefore be considered as data on a society in a pre-crisis situation where tensions were at work under the surface. Our prime concern, however, was to identify and explain some general patterns of social differentiation in two modern socialist societies.

The editors of this volume would like to express their thanks to all the participants in the multinational research project, especially to Mr M. Tucek from the CSSR, Mr L. Király and I. Nemeskéri from Hungary and Mrs S. Walkowska from Poland, for their work on data processing. We would also like to acknowledge the work of Mr J. Szymanderski (Poland) and Mrs A. Bokor (Hungary).

Finally we must thank Margaret Archer and Celine Saint-Pierre for their continuous encouragement.

Budapest-Warsaw
21 March 1981

INTRODUCTION: Theoretical Context

Tamás Kolosi and Edmund Wnuk-Lipiński

Ever since the problem of social inequality became one of the main issues in social thought, philosophers (and later sociologists) have tried to find an answer to the major question: why are people not equal?

Some have seen this as part of the natural social order: inequality is an integral part of the social existence of every human being. In this category we would include certain ancient Greek philosophers (Plato, Aristotle and others), as well as modern functionalists. To them, people are not equal *because* they are living in human society. Society has to be stratified in order to fulfil its basic functions. The functions of society place people in an hierarchical order. We ourselves consider this approach to society as unduly mechanistic.

Other scholars admit that inequality exists in all known types of society. They claim, however, that inequality is the outcome of certain types of economic and social relations. In brief, each stage of development of mankind, or in other words each 'social formation', is characterized by different types of economic relations which produce specific types of social inequalities. But such inequalities are not necessary attributes of all possible types of society. Inequalities may be reduced (or even eliminated) if we abolish the economic relations that generate social inequalities.

Certain specific beliefs underlie this mode of thinking; belief in a classless society and the equal distribution of those traits that differentiate between people in a society. As is well known, such thinking is in the mainstream of the Marxian tradition, although it has had many ancestors in the history of social thought.

Since the Marxian approach plays the role partly of a theoretical system and partly of an ideological doctrine, prevalent in a substantial part of the world, it certainly deserves rather more attention than other streams of social thought about inequality.

The demand for social equality has played a central role in every progressive movement. In most cases, however, the ideals of equality endorsed by these movements were themselves historically constrained. At their debut, each of them sought to eliminate the basic (or what was thought to be the basic) inequality typical of the age. Thus the slaves launched their struggle to do away with the inequality between slave and master in the ancient world; the bourgeois revolutionaries demanded equality with the privileged, though only before the law; and the Utopian socialists wanted to remove inequalities in the ownership of property in a capitalist society. However, at a later point (usually related to the success or failure of the movements), the ideals of equality either became more limited or drifted into the realm of Utopia. As is known, the Marxist movement set as its goal the elimination of the basic social inequality represented by the position of the capitalist and, more widely, the abolition of class societies, characterized by fundamental class differences. Engels, challenging Eugen Dühring's abstract concept of equality, pointed out that 'the idea of equality, both in its bourgeois and proletarian forms, is itself a product of history, created under definite historical circumstances, which again postulate a long historical background. Therefore, equality is "anything but a timeless truth".'[1] Furthermore, Engels wrote with reference to the realistic demand for equality in his own age: 'the realistic content of proletarian equality is the demand for the removal of the classes. Every demand for equality which goes beyond that leads necessarily to absurdity.'[2] This stance adopted by Engels is recognized as the demarcation line between the Marxist and the Utopian approaches to equality.

On the one hand, a reduced ideal of equality and, on the other, a shift towards a Utopian vision emerged in the course of socialist development, too — and here and there such displacements can still be witnessed today. Paradoxically enough, its limitation or shift towards Utopianism have a common conceptual basis, in the assumption that the present (or even an earlier) phase of socialist development provides adequate grounds for the realization of social equality. If that is taken for granted, all that the economic policy-makers appear to have to do is to avoid inequalities and see to it that nobody gets more than the others.

Our social experience has proved that such a policy is Utopian. Despite every effort at social levelling, various latent inequalities re-emerged. At the same time, such policies often involved the limitation of 'genuine' equality. For example, a wage policy aimed at removing wage differentials might result in the replacement of economically necessary financial incentives by fringe benefits which might in fact lead to wider inequalities. This problem is discussed in following chapters. In sum it appears a valid generalization that, if private ownership of the means of production is replaced by collective ownership, some types of inequality are eliminated, some others remain, and some new sorts of inequalities emerge in social life.

Several differences can be observed in the development of the social structure in Hungary and Poland. Details about these are presented in the first chapter of this volume. Here the following key differences should be noted. First, there is considerable variation in the respective condition of the peasantry. Second, and more generally, there is the important difference that from the mid-1960s Hungary embarked upon a major reform in economic and social governance which affected the development of the social structure in many respects, while this had not happened in Poland by the end of the 1970s (i.e., the time at which this research was carried out). It follows that the beginning of the 1970s represented a period of consolidation in Hungary while it was the eve of the outburst of crisis in Poland.

In spite of all these differences, there are many essential common elements in the development of the social structures of the two countries. It is characteristic of both countries (though the peasantry shows differences here, too) that socialist transformation brought an end to the former ruling classes and diminished inherited class inequalities significantly.

While we stress the 'rapprochement' of the major sociostructural groups, we have to recognize that, though the absolute scale of inequalities has fluctuated since the great levelling wave at the turn of the 1940s-1950s, the situation has not changed essentially in the following 30 years. If we compare the difference between population groups in the best and worst conditions, by use of different statistical indices (education, mobility, income, living conditions), we find that these differences have remained unchanged for more than 20 years. Meanwhile, in absolute terms both the best and the worst conditions were of course improving.

It follows from the constant scale of inequality, and from the rapprochement between classes, that differentiation between non-classes has increased. Theoretically, the decrease of differences between classes can be accompanied by an increase in the so-called differences within classes: thus the original sequence of strata remains unchanged while the distances between individual points on this ordinal scale are changing. To date the present investigation has shown that this (though not this alone) has been the case in the last 30 years. Changes in social stratification cannot be taken as changes in the differences within classes alone, for several changes have intersected the traditional class structure and caused new types of differentiation.

Following from moves towards the basic model of socialist development (adopted in Hungary from the end of the 1940s), a social structure has emerged that, on the one hand, reverses features typical of capitalist development: it assures the separation of the 'political state' and 'civil society' and guarantees the autonomy of the political sphere. On the other hand it proscribes the autonomy of capitalist production and unregulated capital relations, replacing them by a planned, centralized redistribution which is determined by the political sphere.[3] Third, it takes equality as one of the basic desiderata of redistribution, that is, the gradual elimination of inherited inequalities, which does not always happen immediately and sometimes has the unintended consequence of leading to newly established sources of inequality.

Here we cannot examine how the new conception was immediately affected, in its very realization, by factors determined by other interests, related to concrete historical circumstances. Nor can we trace through these effects upon its success or the painful tensions they have caused, ultimately influencing later developments. However, it is a well established fact by now that, alongside the primacy of politics, a certain relative autonomy of 'civil society' has survived, or has come into existence again; the centralized, politically determined redistribution was followed by a partial and decentralized redistribution because greater account was subsequently given to considerations of economic rationality. This in turn spelt greater autonomy in commodity production, less precise definition of its function, and some retreat from the ideals of the earlier levelling centralism. The consequence of all these changes is that a multi-dimensional relational system has come into being, where the place of each group in respect to social reproduction is determined by several factors: their place in the field of decentralized redistribution, the position they can obtain in spheres regulated by economic mechanisms (in the labour market and in the 'second economy'), their position *vis-à-vis* inequalities reproduced in the civil sphere (for example, how favourable or unfavourable it is for them to experience sociopolitical intervention through the school system, social policy and other means that challenge spontaneous reproduction).

When we want to outline our 'social structure',[4] we have to analyse exactly what mechanisms govern the relational system just mentioned: (a) how the production of goods takes place in the state and co-operative spheres, what the relationship is between political, state and individual economic units (enterprises, establishments, branches), and what kind of relations it brings into being in terms of the division of labour, sectional interests and power; (b) how those parts of the economy work that are only indirectly regulated, how labour market relations and the possibilities of a 'second economy' modify the situation of different social groups, how the decentralized sector and the sphere regulated by market mechanisms are connected with each other; (c) how the spontaneous reproduction of inequalities happens, what role social origins (broadly interpreted) play in the course of individual and family life; (d) how education, welfare policies, incomes policies and social policy in general can interrupt the spontaneous reproduction of inequalities, and what the effect of such intervention is.

But if we wish to describe the 'stratification' of our society, we must question the results of these mechanisms or processes, examining what kind of differences they introduce between individuals, families or groups, how these differences are linked to one another, how they strengthen or weaken each other's influence, and how they are arranged vertically and horizontally.

Since Max Weber, it is well known in sociology that vertical ranking and horizontal differentiation are generated not only by economic determinants but also by status. The concept of 'social status' is thus considered as another meaningful dimension of social inequality. As Weber put it, status inequality refers to the social prestige (or, using his expression, 'social estimation of honour') emerging from a combination of factors, such as occupation, standard of living, education, social origins, etc.[5] In this volume, however, greater emphasis is placed on objective factors contributing to social status rather than on prestige itself. The concept of social status is a particularly useful analytical tool for the description of our societies in which collective ownership has replaced private ownership in the most significant part of the economy. Furthermore, in such a type of society some market mechanisms are suspended. Hence, traditional class differentiation does not play the same role as in capitalist society.

From the very beginning we have frequently used two terms, 'inequality' and 'equality'; as yet, however, we have not defined the meaning we attach to these concepts. It may seem tedious to define each term in detail, particularly when both are in such common use in sociology, but this seems necessary here for two reasons. First, both equality and inequality are employed in two different contexts; they may be used as scientific concepts or as political ones. Moreover, in some writings these two meanings are mixed and this leads to confusion.

Second, it is vital to be clear in order not to conflate or confuse inequality with heterogeneity. Inequality is connected with hierarchical ordering, with gradations in social positions, while heterogeneity is connected with nominal types of differences.

Both inequality and heterogeneity are two sides of the same coin: social differentiation. Inequality, however, plays an important role in the majority of social and political movements; it generates labour unrest and, in extreme cases, even revolution. That is why this concept simultaneously plays an important role in most ideological doctrines. For this reason 'inequality' has become a slogan, and one that is permanently overused in many different, sometimes quite contradictory, contexts.

In this volume we shall try to use the concept of 'inequality' in a particular strict sense. Following the definition proposed by Peter M.Blau, we understand that 'inequality refers to the distribution of people in terms of status dimensions — how widely they differ in power, or wealth, education or income'.[6] Equally, we accept his statement that 'all social positions that vary by gradation rather than constituting nominal categories are defined as status'.[7] This understanding of social stratification reflects an approach to social structure through the concept of gradation which was earlier developed by S. Ossowski.[8]

This may appear to represent a rather narrow understanding of inequality in comparison with that of C. Jencks and his colleagues.[9] As is well known, not only has Jencks taken into account inequalities stemming from occupational and income status: he and his associates also examined certain social institutions (predominantly the school), the cognitive skills of individuals (and the influence of their genotype on the further social careers of individuals), educational attainments, and even inequality in job satisfaction. Amongst empirical research in the socialist countries, Zsuzsa Ferge takes socio-occupational grouping (defined by division of labour) as the primary expression of social stratification.[10] Csavdar Kjuranow has worked out a specific index of the standard of living as an expression of stratification which he employs in conjunction with occupation, education and income.[11] In similar vein, Pavel Machonin has specified five basic dimensions: (a) socio-occupational status; (b) cultural level of the style of life; (c) education; (d) standard of living; (e) participation in management.[12]

Previous Hungarian and Polish research (which we discuss in detail in the following two chapters) shows almost unanimously that it is socio-occupational status that determines social stratification most strongly in our societies; but nevertheless the whole issue of differentiation can be properly approached only by considering more than one dimension alone.

Hence, the concept of social status is based on the socio-occupational structure, since we accept the premise that, in the socialist type of society, traditional class structure has been replaced largely by occupational strata rather than by any other type of differentiation.[13] So we have taken socio-occupational status as the main variable in our research and we have examined four dimensions of it when analysing inequalities. In the reproduction of inequality, social mobility has great importance, as have working conditions, material living standards and cultural levels. Chapters 1-4 of the present volume deal with the analysis of them in fair detail.

A further problem is presented by the classification of socio-occupational status. We can discover two types of solution in the relevant literature. The one is the classical solution, as worked out by Edwards,[14] based on the nominal grouping of occupations, while the other, from the Gibbs-Martin index[15] to the SIOP scale of Treiman,[16] ranks occupations in hierarchic order with the help of scores based on a combination of objective criteria or on prestige. In our research we have decided in favour of the first variant because we can thereby deal with real social groups. At the same time, the extension of our sample and the differences in international classification did not make it possible for us to employ a highly detailed occupational typology of industrial workers. That is why we have chosen a simple grouping based on the difference between manual and non-manual work and on qualifications. Thus we obtained four main socio-occupational categories:

1. un-skilled and semi-skilled workers;
2. skilled workers;
3. white-collar workers;
4. professional (including managerial) workers.

Usually in the case of 4 we combined the two sections into a single group. Hence, in the majority of our analysis professionals and managers mean one category,[17] though sometimes we were able to make a distinction between them.

We can therefore regard our society as basically hierarchically stratified, where he who holds a better position within the social division of labour usually has a high income, higher social prestige, reaches a higher level of self-accomplishment and is able to shape a more cultural life-style. But the combination of inequalities is neither rigid nor unambiguous, and thus our social stratification is none the less characterized by strong status inconsistencies. Although, since the famous study of Lenski,[18] attention has been paid mainly to the influence of status inconsistency on behaviour, and primarily on political behaviour, in Western countries, it has a greater structural significance in socialist countries.

Not only did the radical political and social changes of the last 35 years result in the breaking down of traditional structures but also, the stratification system was influenced by intersecting effects during this period, and the political efforts to attain equality also produced strong inconsistencies. A considerable part of the population is thus characterized by status incongruence.[19] So when examining inequalities it is of great importance how different types of inequalities combine with each other and what kinds of basic tendencies take shape in the multi-dimensional field of stratification. We have tried to analyse these in the closing chapter of this volume.

At the end of this short presentation of the underlying theoretical premises we would like to touch upon the meaning of equality. This term is very controversial in sociological literature, the hottest issue being whether equality means 'equal opportunities' or 'equal results'. We are not going to discuss these debates because they are well known and basically fruitless. As we indicated earlier, equal results sounds rather Utopian in the light of the experiences of capitalist and socialist societies alike to date. However, if we were to consider 'equal opportunities' as an analytical tool for the measurement of the social situations of different individuals, we would be obliged to take into account the mutual relation between environmental and genetic determinants.

We cannot go as far as that in our deliberations, and when talking about equality, or more precisely convergence, we refer rather to the social situation of certain *groups* — not the relative opportunities of *individuals*.

NOTES

1. F. Engels, *Anti-Dühring*. In *Marx-Engels Werke,* Berlin, 1958, vol. 20, pp. 99 and 581.
2. Op. cit., p. 99.
3. Redistribution is used here not in a narrow economic, but a wider socio-theoretical connection. Cf. Karl Polanyi, *The Great Transformation,* New York, 1944.

4. The notion of social structure is used differently in the specialist international literature, as could be seen at the 69th Congress of the American Sociological Association. Accepting the typology of Peter M. Blau, our conception stands closest to the trend associated with the names of Coser, Blau and Lenski, which interprets the social structure in a given society as a multi-dimensional sphere of differentiated positions of people. Cf. Peter M. Blau's introduction to the 'Approaches to the Study of Social Structure', London, 1976. But at the same time we make a distinction between the notion of structure and that of stratification; by 'stratification' we mean the differentiation of people, while by 'structure' we refer to the social conditions that determine them.

5. M. Weber, 'Class, Status, Party', in *Structured Social Inequality,* ed. Celia S. Heller, New York, 1969, p. 25.

6. P.M. Blau, *Inequality and Heterogeneity,* New York/London, 1977, p. 45.

7. Op. cit., p. 46.

8. S. Ossowski, *Struktura klasowa w społecznej świadomości* (Class Structure in Social Consciousness), Lodz, 1957.

9. C. Jencks, et al., *Inequality,* New York/London, 1972.

10. Ferge Zsuzsa, *Társadalmunk rétegzódése* (Stratification of our Society), Budapest, 1969.

11. Csavdar Kjuranow, *Socialni klas i socialna stratifikacija* (Social Class and Social Stratification), Sofia, 1977.

12. Pavel Machonin (ed.), *Ceskoslovenska spolecnost* (The Czechoslovak Society), Bratislava, 1969.

13. W. Wesołowski, *Z problematyki struktury społecznej: Teoria — Badania — Praktyka* (On the Problems of Social Structure. Theory — Research — Practice), Warsaw, 1975.

14. Alba M. Edwards, *Comparative Occupation Statistics for the United States, 1870 to 1940,* Washington, 1943.

15. J.P. Gibbs and W.T. Martin, 'Urbanization, Technology and the Division of Labour', *American Sociological Review,* 1962, no. 27.

16. Donald J. Treiman, 'Comparative Mobility Measurement', *Social Science Research,* 1975, no. 4.

17. Research in Eastern European countries shows the intense similarity of these two strata, which is also underpinned by historical continuities. The latter is particularly true of the intelligentsia stratum. Cf. in detail the study of Tibor Huszar in Aleksander Gella (ed.), *The Intelligentsia and the Intellectuals,* London, 1973.

18. G.E. Lenski, 'Status Crystallization: Non-vertical Dimension of Status', *American Sociological Review,* 1954, no. 19. For an adequate summary of status inconsistency cf. Sheldam Stryker and Anne Statham Macke, 'Status Inconsistency and Role Conflict', *Annual Review of Sociology*, vol. 4, 1978, (California).

19. The research of Machonin and his collaborators in the second half of the 1960s has shown strong inconsistencies in more than 40 per cent of the Czechoslovak population.

ROOTS OF CONTEMPORARY ISSUES

Chapters 1-4 analyse the results of a comparative investigation focused on selective aspects of the Hungarian and Polish social structure. As both societies have many features in common, from a methodological point of view their comparison seems justified. The social system in both Poland and Hungary is the result of the adoption of the same social and political doctrine. The two countries adopted similar priorities in line with their shared system of values, inherent in the reigning ideology, when aiming at the transformation of their social structure.

Although European socialist societies have many features in common as a result of a social system based on Marxist doctrine, some of these features have their roots in the past. A duality of factors (political and historical) producing similarities is particularly marked in the case of Poland and Hungary, but certain trends in the social structure of the two countries are sufficiently different to be of interest. Although our research work compared internal stratification, concentrating specifically on the social status and the emerging equalities and inequalities of the industrial workers, such factors are determined by the industrialization process and the main development tendencies in the social structure.

As the present cannot be separated from the past, we begin with an historical survey of the industrialization process and social structure of the two countries.

INDUSTRIALIZATION

Ferenc Kovács

At present, Poland and Hungary belong to the economically semi-developed countries, and in this category, according to most indices, they are very similar to each other. Such conclusion can be drawn from statistical data on economic development in the late 1960s and 1970s, for example, GDP per capita,[1] value of net industrial production,[2] ratio of urban dwellers[3] and level of development of the infrastructure.[4]

THE FIRST PHASE OF INDUSTRIALIZATION

In both countries the economic position of semi-development was reached with difficulty. Hungary and Poland until they had regained their national state independence after the Second World War, had existed as independent societies only between the two world wars. This was a very short period out of the past 150 years which were so decisive in Europe for the laying down of the foundations of present economic development. Hungary was part of the Hapsburg Empire, administered from Vienna until 1867; before 1918 it was a politically second-rate and economically third-rate part of the Empire (after Bohemia and Austria). Between 1795 and 1918, Poland was divided among the neighbouring Russian, Austrian and German empires. This meant that the social and economic development of the occupied territories was regulated according to the politics of the different empires. For example, the abolition of serfdom on Polish territories under Prussian occupation took place at the beginning of the nineteenth century. At the start of the twentieth century, 6.5 percent of the population were industrial workers, and the average yield of wheat per hectare was 2.2 tons. On the eastern and central Polish territories under Russian occupation the emancipation of the serfs took place in 1864. At the beginning of the twentieth century in this region, 3.4 percent of the population were industrial workers, and the average yield of wheat per hectare was 1.3 tons. On the south-eastern Polish territories under Austrian occupation, the abolition of serfdom took place in 1848, and around 1910 the proportion of industrial workers amounted to 2 percent and the average yield of wheat per hectare was 1.1 tons.[5]

In both countries, the land-owning gentry class survived until the end of the Second World War, and it had a similar influence on the political and economic life of the two countries. The population was mainly agricultural with an extensive poor peasant class. Although serfdom was abolished in Hungary in 1848, the large estate system was kept — according to estimates, 53 percent of the land remained in the hands of the feudal landowning class. According to data for 1895, about 48 percent of the land belonged to estates larger than 55 hectares.[6] In Poland the situation under the various empires was similar. In 1921, 47.3 percent of the land belonged to estates larger than 100 hectares.[7] The increase in the number of industrial and infrastructural places of work did not counterbalance the agrarian over-population in either country. Between 1870 and 1913, according to estimates, 3.5 million people from Polish territories and 1.9 million from Hungary emigrated — primarily to the USA.[8]

However, the 40-50 years prior to the First World War were of major importance in the economic and social development of both countries. The increasing capitalist industrialization that followed the Napoleonic wars in continental western Europe, was experienced after a delay of about half a century in central and eastern Europe. In Poland and Hungary the agrarian transformation, together with railway building and large industrial initiatives, started a process that was speeded up by the investments of the industrialized western countries and by their food and raw material requirements. By the end of the nineteenth century, the length of rails to every 100,000 inhabitants was 29.3 kilometres (2.9 kilometres for every 100 square kilometres) in the Polish kingdom. In Hungary the same index was 86.6 and 4.8 kilometres. In the UK it was 86 and 10.8, and in Austria 70 and 5.8.[9]

Between 1877 and 1910, the production value of manufacturing industry in the Polish kingdom increased ninefold, but in Hungary between 1898 and 1913 the increase was by a factor of 2.3. In 1913, in Hungary 417,000 workers were employed in manufacturing industry and in 1910 in the Polish kingdom 401,000 were so employed; separate data on Polish territories under German and Austrian occupation were not available.[10]

In the last third of the nineteenth century, therefore, Hungary and Poland simultaneously entered the stage of capitalist industrialization and industrial revolution that brought about a number of fundamental social and economic changes. It had a dynamic effect on society and replaced traditional feudal social relations and their way of life with capitalist relations. It set up a basically capitalist — although not western European-type — social structure. The capitalist class and the industrial working class grew, but the landed class and the poor peasantry existed side by side with them. These two polarized structures were connected by urban and rural middle classes, which thus embodied the contradictions of the two different structures, their heterogeneity and the incompleteness of the industrial revolution.

BETWEEN THE TWO WORLD WARS

Both countries became independent after 1918. When the Hapsburg Empire disintegrated, Hungary became an independent state, but lost two-thirds of her original territory. In both Hungary and Poland, bourgeois governments were set up, which were strongly influenced by the landowning class.

The economy of both countries was heavily affected by the dissolution of the empires, the economic reorganization of the new territory and the reorganization of the national economy in relation to the world market.

In the 1920s agrarian reform was successfully minimized by the landowning class in both countries. As a result there was no significant increase in peasant estates, or in the income of the agrarian population, nor was the demand for increased production or for consumer goods stimulated. The accumulation of capital was low in both countries (estimated at an annual 5-6 percent). The nationalist economic policy of the governments (their efforts to set up an independent national economy) relied, paradoxically, on the import of capital. State loans were floated and opportunities were given for the expansion of foreign private capital. In 1931 Poland's foreign debt per capita was US $35 and Hungary's, US $64. In Hungary the economy only developed slightly as 20 percent of the foreign credit was spent on production, 40 percent on the repayment of debts and 40 percent on the development of the infrastructure or consumption.[11] In Poland, foreign capital took over important parts of industry.[12] In the 1920s in Hungary, 50 percent of the financing of the economy depended on foreign capital, and in 1938 about 25 percent of industrial shares were foreign owned, half of them by Germany.[13]

Industrialization had not developed before the 1929-33 crisis. Only reconstruction and reorganization of certain branches took place (in Hungary, for example, there was a cut-back in the milling industry, but a significant development in the textile industry). The crisis severely affected both countries. In 1932 unemployment was 30 percent in Hungarian industry and, in 1933, 40 percent in Polish industry. By 1936 in Hungary, and in 1937 in Poland, industrial production only matched the pre-crisis level of 1913. In both countries powerful state intervention took place after the crisis.

Industrial development in the second half of the 1930s did not lead to essential industrial and social changes either in Poland or in Hungary, as in the decades before the First World War. In both countries the industrial revolution was not completed.

Hungary's joining the Berlin-Rome axis resulted, for a few years, in advantageous agrarian exports. However, the restraint on industrial development finally led to national catastrophe. Poland fell victim to aggression, and both countries suffered extensive war damage. The extent of the damage was estimated to be 350 percent of the 1938 national income in Poland, and 194 percent in Hungary.[14] Between the two world wars, the population of both countries as well as the ratio of industrial employees considerably increased,[15] but the value of industrial production did not exceed half of that achieved in Czechoslovakia and Austria.[16]

In 1937 the national income per capita was US$100 in Poland, US$120 in Hungary, US$190 in Austria and US$170 in Czechoslovakia.[17] In both Poland and Hungary, the larger part of the national income was the product of agriculture. In 1938 in Poland, 39 percent of the national income was produced by agriculture and

32 percent by industry and construction. In Hungary 37 percent of the national income was produced by agriculture and 36 percent by industry and construction. In Austria the industrial proportion was already 43 percent, and in Czechoslovakia 53 percent.[18] Table 1 illustrates the structure of industry in 1938 (calculated on the basis of production value from manufacturing).[19]

TABLE 1
The Structure of Industry in Poland and Hungary, 1938

	Poland	Hungary
	%	%
Iron and metal engineering	19	29
Industry		
Chemical industry	8	9
Textile, leather and clothing	16	21
Industries		
Food industry	31	29
Other industrial branches	26	12
	100	100

In both countries there was a significant development in the chemical industry and a moderate development in the iron and metal industries, compared to the pre-First World War situation. The food industry in Hungary and the textile industry in Poland were considerably reduced because of the loss of earlier markets. Simultaneously, the Hungarian textile industry and the Polish food industry almost doubled. These shifts (and other technical changes which cannot be analysed here) also altered the composition of the industrial workforce, which in turn brought about definite changes in the life of various sections of the working class. Compared with the pre-First World War situation, which was characterized by the large number of unskilled workers and a few qualified skilled workers (often of a jack-of-all-trades kind), the proportion of skilled workers widened in both countries in the 1930s. A sector of semi-skilled workers, mostly women, appeared, and slowly the proportion of completely unskilled workers decreased.

Before the Second World War, an extensive and highly concentrated industrial working class emerged in both countries, a large part of which was represented by second-generation urban dwellers, fostering working-class traditions. In Silesia, in the Lodz industrial area, and in Budapest there was also an extensive number of third-generation industrial workers.

The slight industrial progress in the period between the two wars did not lay the foundations for significant urbanization or infrastructural development. The infrastructural development of both Hungary and Poland compared with 28 other countries is shown in Table 2. Only a slight change occured in this period of nearly two decades. Although the ranking of both countries improved, they lagged behind the leading countries to a greater extent.

TABLE 2
The Infrastructural Situation of Poland and Hungary 1920-1937

1920		1937	
Order	**Points**	**Order**	**Points**
1. Denmark	75	1. USA	84
21. Hungary	20	20. Hungary	21
23. Poland	16	21. Poland	19
28. Turkey	0.3	28. Turkey	9

Source: Attila Csernok, Eva Ehrlich and György Szilágyi, *Infrastruktura, Korok és Orszábok* (Infrastructure, Ages and Countries), Kossuth, Budapest, 1975, pp. 79, 85.

SOCIALIST INDUSTRIALIZATION

After the democratic coalition, the socialist governments that seized power after the war, on the part of the workers, made the general modernization of their countries and the rapid completion of industrialization their national programme. The first steps were the nationalization of German and collaborationist capital (mines, banks and large estates) and radical agrarian reform. With the further expropriation of capital, the social structure underwent a change. The 'dual structure' (landowners-agrarian proletariats and capitalists-workers) was abolished and the expropriated means of production were placed in the hands of the collectives or of individuals.

This revolutionary transformation occurred in a relatively peaceful manner in both countries during the postwar years. It was facilitated both by the mass of the people and by the help of the Soviet Union. The capitalist-landowner class did not succeed in acquiring any substantial external assistance, and most of the capitalists and landowners left the country during the war.

However, paradoxically, the communist internationalist governments of both countries — based on the current dominant interpretation of Marxism and evaluation of the international situation — were compelled to follow a policy similar to the nationalist development policy of the governments of the 1930s. They wanted to build autarchic national economies, which could be independent from the world market and from participation in the international division of labour. The cold war 'decade' (approximately 1946-59) was the fundamental decade of socialist industrialization. It was the period that strove for autarchy and the primary development of industry, with major emphasis on heavy industry. The economic policy of the 1950s courageously faced the danger of disproportions and risks, but was facilitated by the system of centralized redistribution, in which local and company capital accumulation was used primarily to finance central development programmes. This increasing industrialization not only strengthened the country's regained national independence as a necessary industrial foundation for defence in the cold war international situation, but also furthered the development of the leading class, the working class of the new socialist system.

As a consequence, there was an extremely rapid increase in the size of the working class, primarily of industrial workers in both Poland and Hungary. Between 1950 and 1960, the number of workers employed in nationalized industry increased from 1.9 to 2.9 million in Poland and from 0.8 to 1.3 million in Hungary. The population of Poland increased from 25 to 29.8 million and the population of Hungary from 9.3 to 10 million.[20] During that period the ratio of industrial wage-earners among the active population increased from 20.7 to 25.5 percent in Poland, and from 19.5 to 28 percent in Hungary, while agricultural wage-earners decreased from 54 to 44.1 percent in Poland, and from 52 to 39 percent in Hungary.[21] Naturally, the increase in productivity lagged behind the increase in the labour force, as only a small proportion of the new workers possessed any industrial experience. The huge majority of them came from agriculture or from the home (wives of workers) into industry. (The index of industrial production in 1960, compared with 1950, was 267 in Hungary, while production per capita was only 160.[22]) Nevertheless, from 1950-1960, as a result of structural change, the GDP per capita, in US dollars, increased from $339 to $671 in Poland, and from $234 to $655 in Hungary.[23] There was, therefore, extensive industrial development in both countries.

However, the cost of such development cannot be ignored. The curtailing of consumption affected the entire population, and the reduction of incomes in agriculture affected the majority. Industrial workers were affected by the low standards of real wages, and the development of infrastructural branches of production was deliberately held back. When the impetus for industrialization came to a halt in the mid-1950s, a social crisis emerged in both countries. The revision of the autarchic development policy and the stipulation of targets, which took into consideration contributions from different economic sectors, played an important role in overcoming the crisis. In both Hungary and Poland, increasing attention was paid to the development of infrastructural branches which served the consumption requirements of agriculture and the population in general, accepting a regular increase in living standards.

A new and difficult situation arose when both countries took their places in the international division of labour and the world market. The earlier industrial development and protective sales strategy, backed by the state budget, had ultimately provided security for the new companies and for the various branches of industry, but the lack of competition did not encourage productive efficiency or the fulfilment of consumer requirements. In addition to extensive industrial development, the proliferation of industrial places of work and the building of new plants, other factors had to be taken into consideration, such as profitability, productivity, quality and marketing — all now important parts of the industrial development strategy.

These problems, which have emerged since the mid-1950s, have worried the industrial management of both countries — particularly since the second half of the 1960s. In Hungary a new system of economic management was introduced in 1968. This system changed the earlier practice of planning, control, pricing, sales, development, labour force economy, and the division of company and ministerial functions and responsibilities. The companies, which earlier were the means of accomplishing central plans — were entrusted with realistic economic and entrepreneurial functions. In Poland the WOG (Great Economic Organization) system was introduced in 1973, in which emphasis was placed on the improvement of company economy and increasing company independence.[24] It was experimental in character and shortly after its introduction was slowed down. Later, in Hungary, further changes were made with regard to control and planning in relation to industry. Its aim was to make industry — or the entire economy — capable of responding to price changes on the world market.

By 1973 both countries reached new levels of GDP per capita: Poland attained 46 percent of the US GDP value (compared with 34 percent in 1960) and Hungary achieved 45 percent of the US GDP value (compared with 33 percent in 1960).[25] Compared with the 1950-60 decade, Polish development improved, while the dynamics of Hungarian development slowed down to some extent. It is probable that the increase in Polish industrial production was the most important factor in this improvement, largely owing to the increased number of workers; in Hungary, large-scale organization of agriculture, together with greater emphasis on increased productivity, were more important.

The contribution of industry to the production of national income continued to increase in both countries.[26] The proportion of industrial workers did not grow to the same extent during the same period: in Poland there was an increase from 32.4 to 39.1 percent, and in Hungary an increase from 34 to 42.8 percent (including the building industry). However, productivity of industrial work did improve. In 1978 the productivity index of industry, compared with 1950, was 630 in Poland, and 390 in Hungary.[27]

All these indices show an economic situation of semi-development. However, the living standards of the population and the development of the infrastructure — which are indispensable factors for the regeneration of the workforce and a basic goal of the socialist system — did not keep pace with industrial development. Among other factors, defence played an important role in accounting for this phenomenon.

Compared with 1960, real income per capita rose to a significant extent in both countries: by 1978 it had increased 2.5 times in Poland, and 2.2 times in Hungary.[28] However, in Poland this was coupled with a lessening of supply difficulties and in Hungary with increasing activity in the secondary economy; therefore the quality of life did not improve to the desired extent. This is indicated by the relative stagnation of the infrastructural facilities in both countries shown in Table 3. The table shows that, although both countries improved their situation (expressed in points), particularly when compared with 1937, there was little approach to the standards of the leading country, even though the USA itself had dropped a few points.[29]

TABLE 3
The Infrastructural Situation of Poland and Hungary, 1937-1968

1937			1950			1968		
Order		Points	Order		Points	Order		Points
1.	USA	84	1.	USA	83	1.	USA	78
20.	Hungary	21	20.	Hungary	32	21.	Hungary	34
21.	Poland	19	22.	Poland	28	25.	Poland	29
28.	Turkey	9	29.	Turkey	10	29.	Turkey	14

Source: Csernok, Ehrlich and Szilágyi, op. cit., pp. 85, 87.

Access to the use of the existing infrastructure — the school system, health facilities, etc. — is greater in socialist countries than in capitalist countries, however; and from the second half of the 1960s onwards, there was an acceleration in the development of the infrastructure in both countries. Let us look at some examples. Since 1967, some 60,000-90,000 flats have been built in Hungary every year.[30] In Poland more than 10 million square metres of new flats have been built annually since 1969.[31] Between 1968 and 1978 in Hungary, the number of television sets in households has nearly doubled and the number of car owners has increased almost four times.[32] Similar trends are apparent for Poland.[33] Although indices show that the development of certain infrastructure branches speeded up in both countries, however, only extensive calculations would prove whether the last decade has altered the place of both countries in the rank order of development — and in which direction.

THE STRUCTURE AND TECHNICAL LEVEL OF INDUSTRY

During this century Polish and Hungarian industries have become a force that has determined social changes, while the nature of industry itself — industrial structure, activities and culture — have also undergone fundamental changes. Out of the total 11 or 12 decades of industrialization, the pre-First World War and the post-Second World War decades were the most important periods in both countries, with respect to the earlier development of capitalism and the laying of the foundations for socialism after the war. Industrialization itself has been based on different premises in the socialist period, compared with the period of capitalist industrial development, because of the planned improvement of large industrial companies under state ownership and the subordination of all social resources to the national targets.

These concentrated efforts have produced a relatively extensive and heterogeneous industry in both countries, whose full capacities and flexibility have not yet developed. In both countries extensive material assets and human potential was accumulated in industry, primarily in the large, state-owned companies.

The data in Table 4 clearly illustrate that identical organizational principles have been at work in the industrial structure of both countries — state-owned industrial companies and industrial plants are highly concentrated. State industry can be considered as large industry and cooperative industry as small industry, although there are some small state-owned companies and some large cooperatives.

TABLE 4
Polish and Hungarian Industry

	Poland, 1978		Hungary, 1979	
	State industry	Cooperative industry	State industry	Cooperative industry
Gross value of fixed assets (in billions of national currency)	2,070	69	608	15
Manpower (thousands)	4,022.9	716.8	1,429.3	203.8
Number of workers (thousands)	3,262.6	581.3	1,128.1	198
Graduates (thousands)	160.7		73	
Number of companies	2,862	1,502	702	670
Number of industrial plants (thousands)	9.6	34.8	5.1	4.1
Workers per plant	419	21	280	56
Gross value of fixed assets per plant (in millions of national currency)	215.6	1.98	115.4	3.6
Productive value of fixed assets per worker/gross (in thousands of national currency)	245*	43*	214*	26*

*Gross value of machinery and technological equipment.

Source: Rocznik Statystyczny 1979, GUS, Warsaw, 1979, pp. 159, 144, 145, 162, 166: *Iparstatisztikai Évkönyv,* 1979, pp. 132, 162, 42, 140.

In Poland, in 1978 state industry provided 86 percent of industry's gross production value and in 1979 in Hungary, state industry provided 93 percent of industry's gross production value. Altogether, 84 percent of industrial workers were employed in state industry in both countries.

In the second, so-called complementary,[34] phase of socialist industrialization, which has been taking place from the mid-1960s onwards, greater attention has been paid to the improvement of the regional and production structure of industry. Consequently, industrial development has made considerable progress in the earlier non-industrialized parts of Hungary and Poland, and the branches of heavy industry have been somewhat re-arranged, to the benefit of the chemical industry.

In 1978 in Poland there was an average of 138 industrial workers to every 1,000 inhabitants. However, some significant differences lie behind this average. The biggest concentration was in Lodz, Katowice and Warsaw, where 22 percent of the industrial wage-earners of the whole country were employed.[35] In 1977 in Hungary, there was an average of 157 industrial wage-earners to every 1,000 inhabitants, while in Budapest itself this figure was 225.[36]

The development of the branch structure of industry can be seen in Table 5. In both countries similar trends can be observed. The proportion of heavy industry increased, while that of the textile and food industries decreased. However, almost 30 percent of the industrial workers, with women in the majority, are employed in the latter two branches of industry. In 1978, the proportion of women workers in nationalized Polish industry was 40 percent; it was 45 percent in Hungarian industry, rising to 71 percent in light industry.

In both countries, more than one-third of industrial workers are under 30. Together with the 30-39 age group, they represent 61 percent of the total. Workers aged 55 or older represent only 5-7 percent.

As the data in Table 6 indicate, however, the proportion of young people has decreased and the ratio of middle-aged people (30-40) has increased. This is favourable from the point of view of the growth of a stable and experienced industrial workforce. An even more promising phenomenon has been the rise in educational standards and qualifications. In both countries the multiple-stage trade school system, which trains cadres for industry, has been introduced into the state educational system. According to various

TABLE 5
Transformation of the Branch Structure of Industry

	Poland				Hungary			
	According to gross production		According to size of work force		According to gross production		According to size of work force	
	1938	1960	1978	1978	1938	1960	1979	1979
	%	%	%	%	%	%	%	%
Metallurgy, engineering	19	28.5	43.4	39.4	29	28.7	36.8	38.0
Chemical industry	8	5.6	9.4	6.9	9	7.7	16.0	6.8
Textile, leather, clothing industry	16	15.5	12.3	17.3	21	13.5	9.8	15.7
Food industry	31	26.8	15.4	11.2	29	18.4	18.3	12.1
Other branches	26	23.6	19.5	25.2	12	21.7	19.1	26.5
Total	100	100	100	100	100	100	100	100

Source: Iparstatisztikai Évkönyv, 1979, pp. 31, 34 (at current prices); *Rocznik Statystyczny, 1979,* p. 134 (at 1977 price), p. 145; T. Ivan Berend and György Ránki, *Közép-és Kelet-Európa gazdasági fejlodése a XIX és XX szazadlan* (The Economic Development of Central and Eastern Europe in the 19th and 20th Centuries), Közgazdasúgi és Jogi Kiadó, Budapest, 1976, p. 463.

estimates, mass conveyor belt production systems dominate in the large industries of both Hungary and Poland. These systems entail a detailed division of labour and a massive one-sided concentration on carrying out minutely divided operations. At the same time, there are many jobs requiring versatile skilled workers, and there is an increasing number of fields where automated production is gaining ground. These three different types of historic and technological levels — which co-exist, often within one company — do not have the same manpower requirements, whether in manual and engineering jobs or when considered more generally. They also have different effects on the organization of work, on work

TABLE 6
Manpower in Polish and Hungarian Industries, According to Age Groups

	Younger than 30	30-39	40-54	55-59	60 and older	Total
	%	%	%	%	%	%
Polish industry						
1959	43.1	27.7	22.8	4.4	3.0	100
1977	39.2	22.5	31.4	4.5	2.4	100
Hungarian industry						
1970	40.1	24.4	27.6	5.4	2.5	100
1979	35.1	26.5	32.9	4.8	0.7	100

Source: Jan Szczepański, A szociológas szemével (With the Eye of the Sociologist), Gondolat, Budapest, 1977, p. 47; *Rocznik Statystyczny 1971,* p. 51; *Iparstatisztikai Évkönyv, 1979,* pp. 175-76; 1980 census; detailed data based on the 2 percent representative sample, KSH, Budapest, 1981, p. 99.

discipline and on the system of industrial control and interests. It is not surprising that conflicts exist between these three historico-technical levels in the industries of both countries. Such conflicts can be solved only by the transformation of the average cultural and professional standards of manpower and through comprehensive modernization of industrial production.

The increase in the educational and qualification level of the two countries' industrial workers can be studied in Table 7. A considerable increase has occurred in the educational and qualification level of industrial workers in both countries. The Hungarian data indicate that there was a decrease in the ratio of workers with a basic general education and a larger decrease in the ratio of workers who did not complete primary school. In Hungary, there were 15 percent of unskilled workers, 41 percent of semi-skilled workers and 44 percent of skilled workers.[37] In state industry, the level of qualifications is even better. Here, half of the manual workers were skilled workers and only 12 percent were unskilled workers. With regard to qualifications, there is a major

TABLE 7
Division of Polish and Hungarian Industrial Manpower, According to Educational and Professional Qualification

	High-level education	Medium-level education	Basic professional qualification	Basic general education	Total
	%	%	%	%	%
Poland					
1970	2.6	13	21.9	—	—
1978	3.4	19	29.5	—	—
Hungary					
1970	2.9	14.4	10.2	40.5	68.0
1980	4.4	20.5	19.2	40.1	84.2

Source: Rocznik Statystyczny, 1979, p. 148; 1980 census: detailed data based on the 2 percent representative sample, p. 103.

difference between men and women. In state industry, only 22 percent of the female manual labour force, compared with 65 percent of the male manual labour force, are skilled workers. There is a similar difference in the proportions of semi-skilled workers — 60 percent are women and 25 percent are men. This situation is the result of many factors. In both Hungary and Poland, although women entered industry at the beginning of the twentieth century, 'full' employment of women was only brought about by socialist industrialization. According to social evaluation and public opinion, industry is traditionally not a woman's 'sphere', and therefore women are not encouraged to acquire industrial qualifications. Despite the principle 'equal wages for equal work', wage rivalry between men and women exists and the interests of the male majority predominate. In fact, it is easier to declare a sphere of activity a 'trade' if it involves a majority of men.

The situation is similar in Poland, even if, according to data, the difference is not so conspicuous. In 1978 the proportion of men possessing either basic trade qualifications or medium-level trade qualifications in Polish industry was 49 percent, while that of women was 38 percent.

In the industries and societies of both countries, there is a large percentage of industrial workers who live in the countryside, perserve contact with agriculture through small-scale farming, and commute to urban jobs. In the mid-1970s in Hungary, the proportion of commuters was about one-third in industry; and in the mid-1960s in Poland it was 23 percent.[38] This way of life involves a considerable loss of time, but the supplementary agricultural income is regarded as desirable. Some industrial workers who live in towns are of course involved in food production. This phenomenon has to be considered permanent, as there is no possibility in either Poland or Hungary of settling all workers in close proximity to industrial plants, or of resettling industry nearer the workers.

NOTES

1. Attila Csernok, Éva Ehrlich and György Szilágyi; *Infrastruktura, Korok és Országok* (Infrastructure, Ages and Countries),Kossuth, Budapest, 1975, p. 363.
2. Mieczysław Fleszar, *A'italanos Gazdaságföldrajz* (Universal Economic Geography), Kossuth, Budapest, 1974, p. 61.
3. *International Statistical Pocketbook,* KSH, Budapest, 1978, p. 33.
4. Csernok, Ehrlich and Szilágyi, op. cit., p. 87.
5. Fleszar, op. cit. p. 46.
6. T. Ivan Berend and György Ránki, *Közep-és Kelet-Európa gazdasági fejlödése XIX és XX szazadlan* (The Economic Development of Central and Eastern Europe in the 19th and 20th Centuries), Közgazdasúgi és Jogi Kiadó, Budapest, 1976, p. 62.
7. Fleszar, op. cit., p. 200; Berend and Ránki, op. cit. p. 227.
8. Berend and Ránki, op. cit., pp. 45-6.
9. Ibid., p. 113.
10. Ibid., pp. 174, 178, and Irena Pietrzak-Pawlowska: 'Przewrot przemyslowy', in: *Uprzemyslowienie siem polskich, etc.*, Warszawa, 1970, p. 95.
11. Ibid., p. 323.
12. Fleszar, op. cit., p. 47.
13. Berend and Ránki, op. cit., pp. 332, 398.
14. Ibid., p. 588.

15. Csernok, Ehrlich and Szilágyi, op. cit., p. 342.

16. Berend and Ránki, op. cit., p. 523; Csernok, Ehrlich and Szilágyi, op. cit., p.363.

17. Berend and Ránki, op. cit., p. 422.

18. Ibid., p. 514.

19. Ibid., p. 463.

20. *Rocznik Statystyczny, 1979,* GUS, Warsaw, 1979, p. xxxii; *Hungarian Statistical Pocketbook, 1972,* KSK, Budapest, 1972, pp. 11-12.

21. *A KGST orszagok gazdasaga* (The Economy of the CMEA Member Countries, Collection of statistical data), Statisztikai Kiadó, Budapest, 1979, p. 331.

22. *Hungarian Statistical Pocketbook, 1972,* p. 19.

23. *Economic Bulletin for Europe,* vol. 31, no. 2 (United Nations, NY, 1980) pp. 28-9.

24. *Gábor Róna, Gazdasági partnerünk: Lengyelország* (Our Economic Partner: Poland), Kossuth, Budapest, 1980, pp. 24-7.

25. *Economic Bulletin for Europe,* pp. 29-30; in 1973, according to quoted source, the GDP value was 5,340 per capita in the USA, 2,482 in Poland and 2,433 in Hungary.

26. *A KGST orszagok gazdasaga,* p. 59.

27. Ibid., pp. 49, 53, 311.

28. Ibid., pp. 49, 53.

29. At the same time, Austria, which is not burdened by extensive defence expense because of her neutral status, fell back from the 13th to the 15th place between 1950 and 1960, with regard to her infrastructural level; Austria's number of points changed from 39 to 40, although the GDP per capita increased from 42 percent of the US value to 61 percent during the same period. Czechoslovakia, carrying a heavier defence burden, and where the industrialization and infrastructural improvement of Slovakia took place during the period under review, preserved 18th place in the rank ordering of the countries, and her number of points increased from 39 to 43.The GDP per capita increased from 43 percent of the US value to 58 percent. It seems that there is no connection either between earlier and present economic and infrastructure levels, or between infrastructure levels and defence expenditure. (See Csernok, Ehrlich and Szilágyi, op. cit., p. 87; *Economic Bulletin for Europe*, pp. 28, 30.)

30. *Hungarian Statistical Pocketbook, 1979,* p. 27.

31. *Rocznik Statystyczny, 1979,*pp. xlvi-xlvii.

32. *Hungarian Statistical Pocketbook, 1979,* pp. 28, 29, 30, 31, 122.

33. *Rocznik Statystyczny, 1979,*pp. xlviii, xlix, xlii-xliii.

34. Jan Szczepański, *A szociológas szemével* (With the Eye of the Sociologist), Gondolat, Budapest, 1977, p. 73.

35. *Rocznik Statystyczny, 1979,* pp. lii., 169.

36. *Hungarian Statistical Pocketbook, 1979,* p. 217.

37. József Kepecs and András Klinger. 'The Class and Stratum Stratification of Society in the 1970s', in *Tarsadalmi struk.urank fejlödés* (Development of our social structure), vol. II, p. 253 (TTI, Budapest, 1979).

38. Estimates are extremely difficult because national data are necessarily available according to administrative units and not according to the actual urban nature of residence or place of work. It is even more difficult to compare data on an

international level. Source of Polish data: Szczepański, op. cit., p. 244. Source of Hungarian data: *Manpower Composition and Wage Relations of those Employed in the Socialist Industry* (in Hungarian), KSH, Budapest, 1976, p. 20.

IMPACT ON SOCIAL STRUCTURE

Tamás Kolosi and Edmund Wnuk-Lipiński

Both Poland and Hungary passed through certain common stages in the transformation of their social structures. The early stage of social restructuration occurred in the immediate postwar years. This was characterized primarily by agrarian reform, the expropriation of large feudal estates, the nationalization of industry and the opening up of social mobility channels, particularly to representatives of the working class.

The next stage involved extensive industrialization of the two countries, which led to the emergence of a large industrial working class. In this period, there was a considerable migration of people from the country to the towns, particularly to the new large industrial centres.

After the land reform and the re-allocation of feudal estates to peasant families, agriculture entered the stage of collectivization, implemented by means of heavy administrative measures. In the second half of the 1950s, there was a clearly marked shift in agrarian policy, particularly in Poland. The agriculture of the two countries began to follow two different paths. Hungary continued to nationalize and collectivize her agriculture, although in a more democratic manner, while Poland faced the disintegration of farm production cooperatives, which had been formed under pressures either too weak or strong to maintain them. Rapid return to private ownership followed.

In the 1950s, particularly in towns, the strata of professionals and white-collar workers was steadily growing. Central management in a planned economy had to make use of an extensive bureaucratic machinery, intended to replace market mechanisms. These occupations expanded not only within various authority structures, but also, and perhaps predominantly, at medium and lower levels in industry, in services and in nationalized agriculture. At first, a large part of these strata, perhaps even the majority, consisted of people from the working class, and to a lesser extent of those from the peasantry. With the passage of time, however, this direct channel of social advancement was gradually replaced by the indirect channel represented by various educational establishments (from the people's universities, which ensured an accelerated and superficial advancement in educational development, to actual universities with a normal educational level).

This chapter deals with the development of the main trends in the transformation of social structure, and although the picture is by no means exhaustive, the outline places the present structure in a historical context.

STARTING POINT

The prewar structure of both Hungary and Poland determined the size and direction of social change in both countries. Generally speaking, the structure was characteristic of the early stage of the industrial revolution. The majority of the population earned their living by tilling the soil, and industry was just beginning to emerge from the first stage of its development. According to the 1930 census in Hungary, only 23 percent of the active population worked in industry and 51 percent in agriculture.[1] In Poland, 61 percent of people gainfully employed were peasants, and 26 percent were industrial workers.[2]

At that time both societies had many features in common. The social structure of prewar Poland and Hungary consisted of capitalist and feudal elements. As Ferenc Erdei says, the antagonism between capital and wage labour was intersected by the dichotomy between gentry society and bourgeois society.[3]

Capitalist production, emerging in both societies, had to face a relatively underdeveloped and unevenly developed economy. The diverse strata and groups differed with respect to the organization and culture of production, the nature of consumption, cultural standards, political consciousness and life-style. Hungarian and

Polish capitalism was relatively heterogeneous at its extremes. The ruling class consisted of the gentry of feudal origin, while the capitalist class was a part of the new bourgeois society that had emerged as a result of the industrial revolution. At the bottom of the social hierarchy there was the peasantry, in an early phase of differentiation, and a comparatively thin stratum of industrial workers which formed a more organic part of the bourgeois society.

EARLY STAGE OF SOCIAL RESTRUCTURING

As K.M. Słomczynski and W. Wesołowski point out, 'In socialist countries, economic decisions derive from political decisions, and, therefore, transformations of the class structure are also largely due to political decisions.' As the various social mobility channels were affected, they argue:

> The labour market was controlled by the state and thus the government could, at various periods of time, introduce specific channels through which individuals could move between the classes. For instance, towards the end of the forties and in the early fifties, a considerable number of workers passed into the managerial class. This was obviously due to political rather than economic factors.[4]

Land reform is another example of a political decision that caused basic social changes. Under the terms of the March 18th Decrees of the Provisional Government, large feudal estates were expropriated in Hungary and later the land was allotted to over 600,000 families. Ninety percent of the people who acquired land were agricultural labourers. A proportion of these people had a strong connection with the working class and later, because of a change in the economic conditions of agriculture, were relatively well disposed to give up their land and either go back to the factory of join the newly established cooperatives. As a result of the agrarian reform in Hungary, the ratio of agricultural workers or landless peasants decreased, between 1930 and 1949, from 23 to 8 percent, while that of the small rural producers (individual farmers) rose from 25 to 39 percent.

Postwar territorial changes in Poland were the main cause of the difference in the development of agrarian reform in the two countries. The changes resulted in considerable relocations of the population from the eastern to the western and northern territories. R. Turski says:

> as a result of the land reform, the rural population from the 'old' territories (excluding territories regained in 1945) was alloted 2,384,400 hectares of land, of which 1,890,300 hectares were used for new farms and 494,100 hectares for the extension of the existing ones. This acreage was taken over by 347,100 new and 254,400 enlarged farms. Every fourth farm on the 'old' territory in 1949 took advantage of the agrarian reform. Change wrought by the agrarian reform from the point of view of the peasantry's agrarian structure was considerable. While farms below 2 hectares and above 20 hectares (the extremes) became fewer in number, small-size (2-5 hectares) and particularly, medium-size farms, grew.[5]

The agrarian reform in Poland promoted the 'levelling' of farms as regards their acreage, and consequently reduced stratification within the peasantry. The existence of a large number of dwarf (2-5 hectares) farms, accompanied by the growing demand for unskilled and semi-skilled workers in towns, produced the social phenomenon that Polish sociologists call peasant workers. The phenomenon was not transitional in nature, as the number of peasant workers has remained at the level of approximately 1.5 million people for many years.

Nationalization of industry in both countries continued. The process of nationalizing all economically important branches of industry and services came to an end in the late 1940s. Iván T. Berend[6] points out that, having set up a well-functioning system of state intervention in the initial phase of the revolution, when the main objective was the stabilization of the economy, the Hungarian Communist Party succeeded in nationalizing the key units of the capitalist sector. The process was slow and gradual. In 1949 plants with more than ten workers were expropriated, with the result that the majority of workers came to be employed in the socialist sector. There was a slight increase in social mobility during the initial stage of transforming the administrative employees and professionals. The training of the so-called 'working intelligentsia' (people of working class and peasant origin) started in the newly founded people's colleges and in universities. A very large number of workers and peasants were raised to managerial posts without any professional training, or after only a short preparatory course. This political decision covered the entire nationalized sector of the national economy in both countries. In Hungary, at the helm of every second nationalized enterprise there was a worker-turned-manager. Every tenth worker (about 60,000 people) had been thus promoted by the end of 1948.[7] Similar trends appeared in Poland.

Although the first revolutionary measures were primarily political, they had many side-effects, some predictable and some unpredictable. The long awaited land reform in 1945 constituted social support for the power of peasants, but it soon became the main obstacle for another political act — the collectivization of agriculture. At this time in Poland there was no change. Generally speaking, all political acts were subordinate to the main strategic target: the building of socialism and the introduction of an entirely new social system. Political acts should, therefore, be evaluated in terms of the practical application of a general revolutionary theory rather than as mere acts of social policy.[8]

In Hungary and Poland, the system of social management and central planning subordinated all available societal and economic resources to the centre. If contemporary concepts are employed, it can be said that the sources of development were the reduction of industrial production costs, the increased tax burden on agriculture and the traffic of goods.[9]

Strenuous efforts were made to concentrate industry, while small-scale production was discouraged, and surplus agricultural produce as well as its work-force were directed towards industry. By keeping living standards and the consumption of the population at a comparatively low level, both countries were able to launch major investment projects. They were also in a position to compel women to seek employment, which was part of the political programme of female emancipation. As a direct consequence of these processes the number of people employed in industry rose extremely rapidly. From 1948 to 1954 the number of industrial workers in Hungary rose by 55 percent and the number of administrative staff increased by 140 percent. In the same period in Poland the number of industrial workers rose by 66 percent.[10]

Such changes were connected with the migration from the country to the towns, which in the late 1940s escalated in both Poland and Hungary. According to the census, between 1946 and 1950 the Polish rural population decreased by 1.1 million.[11] In Hungary between 1948 and 1952 about 300,000 people abandoned agriculture because of forced collectivization, which was instituted mainly through administrative measures — by high taxes imposed on individual farms, for example, and an unfavourable system of purchasing agricultural products. On the other hand, extensive industrialization offered employment in urban centres and was ready to absorb thousands of newcomers. The transformation of the social structure in the two countries was determined by the political doctrine adopted, but the political application of this doctrine involved the manipulation of large masses of people. Later this manipulation was seen to have contained many errors. As Z. Ferge points out,

> the arbitary interpretation of the course of the social revolution was both the cause and the consequence of the dictatorial character of the social leadership in the 1950s. The leaders thought themselves infallible in theory and in practice: history was made to conform to their assumptions and they could not err in their decisions. If, however, things were going wrong, two solutions could be envisaged. Problems could be ignored (that is why social research, including sociology or detailed social statistics, was not called for, and in fact, was almost entirely suppressed); alternatively, difficulties could be imputed to the underhand scheming of internal or external agents who had to be fought by any means. The atmosphere of the cold war, of course, helped to prove the necessity of dictatorial action of this kind.[12]

The historical period of the 1950s, often defined as the period of 'constructing the foundations of socialism', left a permanent mark on the social structure of both countries. The nationalization of all the most important sectors of the national economy, the collectivization of agriculture and the full control of the whole national economic system enabled the authorities to determine the further development trends of the two countries centrally. This central decision-making was administrative in nature; that is, it operated through manipulating market mechanisms.

As a result of the forced and extensive expansion of industry (primarily heavy industry), the number of workers and administrative employees in industry and construction nearly doubled, while in agriculture the labour force was reduced. At the same time, the transformation of small-scale peasant farms into large-scale units was the beginning of a new economic and social situation in agriculture. Because of a certain amount of economic development, together with a higher degree of societal change, the number and percentage of non-manual workers showed a marked rise. New professional and white-collar strata emerged, primarily recruited from workers and peasants and their children.

What was the result of the transition from manual to non-manual work? To a smaller degree in traditional professional jobs, and to a larger degree in managerial posts in the economy and politics, the old strata were partially replaced by a new one.

On the other hand, owing to centralization, technological advance and the societal changes, the stratum of administrative employees grew in number. Here the historical context becomes important, as there was a difference between the managerial stratum before and after 1956 (a political and social turning point in both countries). Before 1956 a worker-turned-manager did not become a true professional even given the required qualifications: the worker-turned-manager and the traditional manager stood apart in every respect. Owing to the new societal policy, the situation of the managerial stratum changed considerably after 1956.

Expertise became an increasingly valuable asset in government, politics and management, and the differences between the 'new' professional and the 'old' professional became increasingly less important, both from a political and a social point of view.

After the social changes in the 1940s and the first half of the 1950s, which were similar in both countries, certain significant differences, deriving primarily from the process of nationalizing production, began to emerge in the further evolution of the social structure in Hungary and Poland. Hungary continued to follow the same pattern, but after 1956 collective farms in Poland collapsed and there was a return to private ownership. In addition, private handicraft work and trade returned. In the first half of the 1960s, 96 percent of the active population in Hungary and 58 percent in Poland worked in the nationalized economy.[13] However, 94 percent of workers employed in the Polish private economic sector were individual farmers. The difference is, therefore, mainly one of the extent to which agriculture was nationalized in the two countries. In the first half of the 1960s, at least, similar processes could be observed in industry. The necessity of shifting from an extensive to an intensive method of economic development not only slowed down large-scale social reconstruction, but created new socioeconomic conditions. The forced and extensive industrial expansion was accompanied by the emergence of a socioeconomic system of management, which was highly centralized. However, it became clear that this system was inadequate for the attainment of the objectives of intensive economic development. Practical measures were then taken in several areas. Greater leeway was allowed for the spontaneous ebb and flow of money and goods, and efforts were made to decentralize public administration and economic management. The system of compulsory central planning was partially replaced by management through economic regulators, and greater scope was given for freer interplay between various institutions, production units and members of the population. It was a controlled process, but not one solely directed from the centre.

New tendencies in the evolution of the social structure were promoted by the depletion of resources entailed by an extensive type of economic development and a new system of socioeconomic management — the results of a type of development that mainly employed indirect methods. The Marxist formula, that ownership of the means of production is the basic factor in social structuration, was seen to be inadequate with regard to the social situation in both countries. Marxist sociologists, therefore, faced a theoretical dilemma, which they tried to solve in various ways. W.Wesołowski, who represents such a school of thought, says:

> the evolution of the class structure in socialist societies involves the gradual standardization of the attitude of various groups towards production and simultaneously a gradual reduction of the part this attitude plays in determining other features of social position and the content of social consciousness. As a result, the differentiating role in society is more and more often played by aspects of social position, such as character of work, income, education, prestige and so on. In socialism these features retain their 'autonomous' life. Although the developed socialist society is classless, we have to acknowledge social differentiation which can be called stratification.[14]

Many sociologists began to search for new stratificational factors, which would more fully explain the transformation of the social structure in socialist societies. J. Szczepański says:

> While describing a capitalist society, a Marxist faces an easier task, since he has at his disposal such class division criteria as the attitude towards the means of production and the share in the national income, etc. In the post-capitalist society, however, where at least a part of the means of production is nationalized, or in the socialist society with no private means of production, the above-mentioned criteria are no longer valid. In this case it is possible to make use of various combined criteria and divide people into classes and strata according to education, income, occupational position and other features.[15]

Consideration of these various criteria for the description of social structure in the 1950s and late 1960s resulted in many investigations being conducted into the differentiation of Polish and Hungarian societies. These investigations made it possible not only to observe general changes in the social structure, but also to trace through differentiations occurring within the manual and non-manual strata. Investigations carried out in the late 1950s and the first half of the 1960s[16] found a markedly hierarchical structure, where certain peculiarities of status within the social division of labour proved to be strong stratum-forming factors. This stratified structure and its resulting social differences could most readily be described in terms of socio-occupational groups.

At that time no one considered that the hierarchical system could be eliminated, but at least none of the strata were homogeneous, and overlapping was rampant. During the past 15 to 20 years, there have been major changes in the structure of the division of labour. In keeping with technological progress, the nature of manual and non-manual work has been converging. However, this does not mean that the differences have become less marked between a creative or managerial job and heavy manual labour. The convergence can be best seen where manual and non-manual work are adjacent in the middle of the distribution — the intermediate area embracing them has broadened and their contours have blurred. This tendency has been facilitated by technological advance, the uneven development of industrial manpower, and a restructuration of the production sector. An initially slow influx of manpower into the service sector, where most manual and non-manual jobs are very similar to each other, started in the late 1960s.

The nationwide transformation of the division of labour has to take into consideration new developments in the division of labour between the sexes. When economic development was extensive, women sought employment in large numbers. During the change-over to the intensive type of economy, the proportion of women entering employment slightly decreased, but between 1960 and 1978 in Hungary the number of male earners declined by 250,000 and the number of female earners rose by 500,000. Between 1960 and 1976 in Poland, the number of male earners (in the nationalized sector of the economy) increased by 1,977,600, while the number of female earners rose by 2,711,400. By 1960 women constituted a third of the total labour force in both countries. By 1978 women constituted almost half the workforce in Hungary and 43 percent in Poland.

However, the increase in female employment affected mainly the semi-skilled and unskilled jobs in industry. Women constitute 19 percent of the skilled workers in Hungary and 50 percent of the unskilled and semi-skilled workers; 50 percent of the manual workers of the agricultural cooperatives in Hungary engaged in farm labour are men and 80 percent are women. Men tend to have higher qualifications, and women, in the main, are tillers of the smallholding and auxiliary plots. The process of 'depeasantization' — the giving up of traditional peasant activities — is slower among women.

The social context of the two countries was in many ways similar over the past 15-20 years, but significant differences were connected not only with a different situation in agriculture. The similarity of certain general social processes does not mean that they take place in the same political and economic conditions. The clash of similar social processes in different economic and political contexts has produced significant differences in social consciousness.

Both in Poland and in Hungary, education has become one of the most important channels of social mobility: it enables people to raise their social status in accordance with the generally accepted system of values. It is therefore obvious that education has become one of the main aspirations of the younger generation. The demand for even higher educational attainments at both the national and individual levels has boosted the level of qualifications in every field. Though economic prosperity partly provided a basis for meeting these demands, the system of the division of labour could not keep pace with the sharp upgrading of educational standards. A related development was an increased differentiation among people who, in general terms, worked in similar occupations, such as engineering and teaching. As a consequence, the old connection between education and work has loosened. As a by-product of this process, the 'lower' brackets of the highly qualified came closer to the higher brackets of the lower qualified than in the past. Now school-leavers with qualifications identical to those of prior generations take up different careers. There are, of course, differences among the various trades, and, owing to the expansion of the training of skilled workers and the advance of specialization in various trades, these differences have increased over the past 15 years. The stratum of skilled workers shows the biggest differences statistically but similar phenomena can be seen among college and university graduates even though the differences between them are slighter.

The demand for higher education and training qualifications runs contrary to the requirement of technological advance for more semi-skilled manual or routine non-manual workers. For many people the consequence of these processes is that their training and formal status put them in a higher social bracket than their actual job.

At the same time, however, the technological leap, characteristic of both countries, particularly in the 1970s, has produced significant changes in production conditions. The Hungarian economic system was essentially different from the Polish system as it was characterized by a decidedly greater flexibility, a higher degree of decentralization and compliance with market mechanisms. The Hungarian system, therefore, was more capable of absorbing new production techniques and work organization systems. In Poland, the import of production engineering was not accompanied by a growing flexibility of the economic structure. The highly centralized economic management, with practically no mechanisms for independent social control, resulted in individual economic units being incapable of carrying out central decisions. Such decisions led to growing discontinuities in economic development and to debts abroad (not submitted to social control). As a consequence, the lengthy economic slump during the second half of the 1970s resulted in a social and political crisis in 1980.

ESSENTIAL FEATURES OF RECENT SOCIAL DIFFERENTIATION

The present-day structure of Polish and Hungarian societies is most often described by means of three (textbook-like) analytical categories. We refer to industrial manual workers, the peasantry, and the non-manual workers, and analyse mutual relations between these three sections and study their internal differentiation.

As the structure of Hungarian and Polish agriculture is essentially different, the characterization of present-day social differences in the two societies with regard to agriculture should be given serious consideration.

In Hungary, the past 15-20 years have seen a radical

transformation of the peasantry, given their exodus from peasant-agricultural work in the period of extensive development. The land reform, however, was accompanied by a strengthening of the peasant character of the agricultural population — a kind of 're-peasantization'. In the 1950s, when masses of peasants left agriculture, the status of the peasantry was destabilized. However, the departure from agriculture did not mean immediate de-peasantization. Certain peasant features were preserved, as most of the peasants-turned-workers continued to live in rural areas, other members of the family remained as agricultural earners, and many of the 'new' workers were still active on the household and auxiliary plots. During the past 15 years, the peasant character of these features has faded and workers of peasant origin have become part of the industrial manual stratum.

The majority of the peasant population that continued to work in agriculture now work in cooperatives, and a small percentage work on state farms. Despite the fact that they are 'wage-earners', the status of the state farm workers has always been halfway between that of the industrial workers and of the peasantry. In the 1940s and 1950s most of the manual workers on the state farms had peasant characteristics, but in the 1950s and 1960s, because of the commercial character and high technological standards of the state farms, there was a marked tendency towards de-peasantization. Peasant features faded further, and the characteristics of workers were strengthened by various developments. The work force on the state farms changed with regard to both its structure and its training; the wage system was remodelled; there was a great advance in technological development; and working hours became shorter. At the beginning of the 1960s crop cultivation and animal husbandry were modernized. Paradoxically, in certain groups of state manual workers, peasant characteristics have been retained to a greater degree than among the peasant-turned-non-agricultural worker. However, even here the process of de-peasantization has started, with the result that these groups have become integrated with the industrial workers.

The change-over from small-scale production of private farms to large-scale production on cooperative farms has triggered off a kind of de-peasantization process. However, in the early 1960s it seemed to be more practical to preserve peasant characteristics within the cooperatives for an extended period of time.

Then, as a result of the new developments that started in the mid-1960s, the cooperative peasantry increasingly lost its traditional characteristics, as cooperative members started to become industrial workers. The cooperatives became increasingly commercialized in nature, work was modernized, and a new generation grew up. Traditional peasant activities were gradually replaced by specialized skilled and semi-skilled labour, and the rate of occupational mobility was high among the cooperative workers. They secured access to the national labour market with accompanying and significant changes in their way of life and consumer habits.

In Polish agriculture, the second half of the 1950s brought about a radical change. After a period of intensive collectivization, the farms again came under private ownership. Today over three-quarters of the gross agricultural output comes from individual farming and only one-fourth from nationalized farming (state-owned farms and cooperatives). Several changes took place.

1. There was a growth of commodity production in individual farming. At the beginning of the 1950s, commodity production was approximately 50 percent of the output from individual farming, but by 1976 it had increased to 83 percent. There was a gradual departure from traditional autarchic forms of production and a movement towards market production.

2. Industrialization of agriculture was accompanied by the growth in commodity production — primarily owing to mechanization and intensification of agricultural production (use of machines, chemical fertilizers, etc.).

3. The professionalization of work in individual farming began to occur. Farming ceased to be a way of life and increasingly assumed the features of a trade. This process resulted from the industrialization of farm production and the rising level of education (specialized and general) among younger farmers.

4. The urban life-style gradually spread into the country areas. This phenomenon, observed as early as the 1960s, is often termed the 'social urbanization of the countryside'. Individual farmers now increasingly aim to reach urban living standards in terms of housing conditions, consumption patterns, etc.

5. There is a migration of peasant youth from the countryside to the towns — in spite of the other processes taking place. W. Nowak says:

> Investigations show that migrants from the countryside are better educated. This applies not only to peasant migrants, but also to people who, while living in the countryside, are occupationally active outside their farms. Young peasants often regard their education in elementary schools as the opportunity to enter fields other than agriculture.[17]

Qualitative changes and internal differentiation followed the expansion of the industrial workforce. In the period of the extensive development of the economy industrial workers were differentiated, but that differentiation was slight and of minor significance. According to M. Jarosińska and J. Kulpińska,

> Among present-day industrial workers there is an increasing number of 'original workers', that is, those who have belonged to this class for at least two generations. A large percentage of the young workers' fathers came to the towns in the 1940s and 1950s, and the influx of their children into industry made the present-day worker culturally uniform and stable. The basic difference between fathers and sons is the way they started work and acquired qualifications. While the fathers were mainly trained at work, their sons attended technical schools.[18]

Education and professional qualifications are not the only factors that differentiate industrial workers. Although an increasing number of workers have acquired qualifications and there has been a rise in the level of general education (in both countries, among the under-30s over one-third of those with secondary school education work as skilled workers), the impact of technological progress, the consolidation of the new form of work organization, living conditions and the slow but steady transfer of workers into the tertiary sector are also factors that have to be taken into consideration. A particularly important factor for Hungary is the place of residence, as over half the workers live in rural areas.

Until the second half of the 1970s there appeared to be no slowing down of the massive restratification occurring among the white-collar workers. W. Makarczyk and J. Bluszkowski assess that, in Poland,

> white-collar workers account for about one-third of all workers employed in the nationalized economy. The comparative analysis of the successive personnel registers indicates a relatively weak, but distinctly marked, growth of this stratum's share in the total population employed in the nationalized economy. The percentages of white-collar workers in selected years were: 1958, 31.2%;

> 1964, 33%; 1968, 34.2%; 1973, 34.6%; 1974, 35.4%. The difference of 4.2% is far from significant. However, the numerical growth of this stratum is more striking as in the investigated period the number of white-collar workers doubled. The difference amounted to about two million workers.[19]

In Hungary, between 1949 and 1963 the number of white-collar workers increased by 140 percent and the increase in the next 15 years was 15 percent. However, the difference in percentage is due to a difference in methods of calculation. In both periods, the increase represented a gain of half a million people, an increase accompanied by a marked internal differentiation. During the past 15-20 years there has been a rise in the status of professionals and a fall in that of white-collar workers.

In both countries, the differentiation of white-collar labour has included a growth in the number of people in simple and routine work. The wages of subordinate white-collar workers are below the national average.

As a result of these factors, subordinate white-collar workers constitute an occupational category rather than a self-contained stratum. Some objective differences in the working conditions of office workers and blue-collar workers give credibility to the view that there is a demarcation line between the two. Subordinate white-collar workers are only a specific stratum, as a review of family background, related living conditions and social position reveals that they are similar to manual workers in, for example, commerce, services and other branches of the economy.

However, medium-level white-collar workers constitute one of the most heterogeneous strata of society. It is difficult to distinguish them from other workers in two respects. There is hardly any difference between the lower stratum of medium-level technical experts, who have a medium level of education, and foremen (who are usually classified as manual workers) or the upper stratum of skilled workers, who have grammar school qualifications. With regard to the character of their work and family relations, the lower stratum of medium-level white-collar workers hardly differs from the upper stratum in commerce and services.

A large group of medium-level experts also overlaps with the lower reaches of the professionals. They could be perhaps termed 'semi-skilled professionals', as their work demands intellect. *Mutatis mutandis,* their qualifications and the nature of their work can be compared to those of people in higher professional work, just as semi-skilled workers, in the classical sense, can be compared to skilled workers. As far as their family and social relations are concerned, this group of medium-level experts is linked primarily with professionals and secondarily with the worker elite. The value orientations of this group are most similar to those of professionals.

As a result of the increased differentiation of non-manual workers, professionals have been distinguished from the subordinate white-collar stratum, and there is a differentiation within the stratum itself. In our definition, professionals constitute the stratum of people whose jobs require college or university qualifications. The separation of professionals from other white-collar workers is the result of a merger between professional and managerial functions, an increased regard for expertise, and a change in political approach. There has also been a general increase in the national demand for highly qualified experts. With the advent of indirect methods in the management of society, professionals at various levels of the institutional structure have been given more elbow room, and within the context of 'to each according to his work', expectations about rewards vary with the qualifications and post of the individual.

At first sight the internal differentiation of non-manual workers appears to run contrary to the separation of the professionals. However, within the professional stratum subordinates are in a less favourable situation than superiors, college graduates than university graduates, graduates of an evening correspondence course than day-release graduates, people with a family background of manual work than people with a background of non-manual work, and people from Budapest than people from the provinces. Similarly, a teacher is in a less favourable position than a doctor, and a legal advisor is in a less favourable position than a lawyer. People who cannot find access to the secondary economy are at a disadvantage to those people who find it a lucrative source of income; men are better off than women; and young people are in a better position than the middle-aged. The disadvantages and advantages on the various dimensions accumulate and generate major differences in socioeconomic positions. The difference between, for example, a female teacher of history, who graduated from an evening course, works in a rural community and comes from a manual worker's family, and the head of a department in a

Budapest hospital, who comes from a professional family, can exceed the differentiation within any of the stratum.

All these changes show two parallel tendencies in Hungarian structural development: there is a convergence of classes, and there is a lessening of the differences between the strata. Occasionally there is an elimination of particular differences and an increase in other forms of stratum-related differentiation.

NOTES

1. Such a proportion could be found, for instance, in Germany in the second half of the last century.

2. W. Wesołowski and K. Słomczyński, *Investigations on Class Structure and Social Stratification in Poland,* Warsaw, 1977, p. 54.

3. Ferenc Erdei mentioned this dichotomy. Although the development of the structure of Hungarian society before its liberation in 1945 and since then has remained a controversial issue, detailed discussion of it goes beyond the scope of this chapter. In our opinion, a lecture jointly written by Péter Hanák, Miklós Laczkó and György Ránki and delivered during the preparation for the ten-volume *History of Hungary* was most convincing. See *Vita Magyarország kapitalizmuskori fejlödéséröl* (Debates on the Development of Hungary in the Capitalist Era), Budapest, 1971.

4. Wesołowski and Słomczyński, op. cit., pp. 54-5.

5. R. Turski, 'Przemiany klasy chłopskiej', in W. Wesołowski (ed.), *Kształt struktury spolecznej,* Wrocław, 1978, s. 48-9.

6. Cf. T. Iván Berend, *Ujjáépités és a nagytöke elleni harc Magyarországon 1945-48* (Reconstruction and Struggle against Large Capital in Hungary between 1945 and 1948), Budapest, 1962. Another work that analyses this period is Ránki György, *Magyarország gazdaságaaz elsö 3 éves terv idöszakában* (Hungarian Economy during the First Three-year Plan Period), Budapest, 1963.

7. Estimates put the number of manual workers promoted to managerial posts from 1949 to 1954 at about 250,000. However, a small percentage of them worked as managers for a short period and then were redirected to manual labour.

8. Z. Ferge, *A Society in the Making,* New York, 1976, p. 61.

9. The topic was mentioned, for example, by Ernö Gerö on 27 November 1948: cf. Ernö Gerö, *Harcban a szocialista népgazdáságért* (Efforts to Build a Socialist People's Economy), Budapest, 1950, pp. 298-301.

10. *Rocznik Statystyczny 1977,* Table 1, s. xxxvi.

11. *Rocznik Statystyczny 1972,* Table 1/35, s. 68.

12. Ferge, op. cit., p. 63.

13. *Rocznik Statystyczny 1972,* Table 1/71, s. 107.

14. W. Wesołowski, *Klasy, Warstwy, Władza* (Classes, Strata, Authorities), Warsaw, 1966, s. 185-6.

15. J. Szczepański, *Odmiany czasu teraźniejszego* (Variants of the Present Time), Warsaw, 1973, s. 706.

16. In Hungarian sociological literature an outstanding work is Zsuzsa Ferge, *Társadalmunk rétegzödése* (The Stratification of our Society), Budapest, 1969. In Polish sociological literature mention should be made of J. Szczepański (ed.), *Z badań klasy robotniczej i inteligencji,* (Investigations on Working Class and Intelligentsia), Łódź, 1958;J. Szczepański (ed.), *Studia nad rozwojem klasy robotniczej* (Studies on the Development of the Working Class), vols. I and II, Łódź, 1961 and 1962; W. Wesołowski (ed.), *Zróznicowanie społeczne* (Social Differentiation), Wrocław, 1970.

17. W. Nowak, 'Przemiany klasy chłopskiej', in W. Wesołowski, (ed.), *Kształt struktury społecznej* ('Transformation of the Peasant Class', in *The Shape of Social Structure),* Wrocław, 1978, s. 101.

18. M. Jarosińska and J. Kulpińska, 'Czynniki położenia klasy robotniczej', in W. Wesołowski (ed.), *Kształt struktury społecznej* ('Factors of the Working-Class Position', in *The Shape of Social Structure),* Wrocław 1978, s. 110.

19. W. Makarczyk and J. Bluszkowski, 'Przemiany warstwy pracowników umysłowych', in W. Wesołowski (ed.), *Kształt struktury społecznej* ('Transformation of the White-Collar Stratum', in *The Shape of the Social Structure*), Wrocław, 1978, s. 180.

1

MOBILITY AND SOCIAL RELATIONS

György Akszentievics

The term 'mobility' refers to the shift of an individual from one socio-occupational category to another through a change of occupation. As this survey is restricted to industrial workers, only their so-called 'entrance mobility' is examined.

A high level of mobility is regarded as desirable for two reasons. It enables the members of the lower level in the social hierarchy to rise, and it ensures against the isolation of the socio-occupational categories, the stiffening of the social structure or the development of castes (which is not considered desirable in a socialist society).

However, the mobility process is regarded differently from the point of view of individual and social interests. In general, a rise in the social hierarchy is clearly favourable for the individual, but the effect on society varies. It is usually advantageous both for society and the individual for a significant percentage of individuals to rise in the social hierarchy, as such upward mobility is accompanied by social and economic development.[1] Social interest usually clashes with individual interest in the case of downward mobility. It is in the interest of society that low-prestige, badly paid and heavy manual work should be carried out within the division of labour, but it is in the interest of a large percentage of people engaged in such work to rise in the social hierarchy. When some of them succeed, there is, as a consequence, a shortage of labour in the jobs they have left.

In the social division of labour, it is in the interests of society that the most suitable individuals should work in the most important posts. This occasionally requires, or presumes, that more suitable people will replace the less suitable. Both the shortage of labour occurring with regard to low-prestige jobs, and the 'qualitative replacement' of those engaged in important jobs, therefore, require a certain amount of downward mobility. Here, as in most cases, as far as the individual is concerned, a rise would be more favourable. This contradiction can only be solved in the long term, given a much higher level of general, scientific and technical development.

A change of occupation to another on the same level in the hierarchy is not regarded as social mobility; such horizontal exchange of occupation takes place for multitudinous reasons, and has various effects on both the individual and society.[2]

As our research aimed at comparing the general situation of the industrial socio-occupational categories alone, the data concerning mobility are limited. Another difficulty in comparing mobility was the chronological discontinuities, in the historic and economic development of the two countries. In Hungary there were considerable geographic changes of frontier at the beginning of the 1920s which affected the mobility projections from the grandfathers, and to a lesser extent the fathers, of the respondents. In Poland similar frontier adjustments took place about 25 years later; these affected not only the fathers, but also a significant proportion of the respondents themselves. A similar example can also be found with regard to agriculture, where collectivization took place only in Hungary and cannot even be expected to take place in Poland in the near future.

The survey examines the connection between the first and present occupation of the respondents (intra-generational mobility); the composition of the four industrial socio-occupational categories according to their family background; and the development of the occupational data in their totality. Occupational data on spouses and wage-earning children and the connections between the occupation of the respondent and his/her close family circle were also taken into account.

INTRA-GENERATIONAL MOBILITY

In spite of the fact that social changes during the first decades of socialism were more extensive in Hungary than in Poland, because of the change accompanying the transformation of agriculture, intra-generational mobility of the two manual categories is greater in Poland.[3] White-collar workers are more mobile in Hungary, while professionals show the same degree of mobility in the two countries.

In both countries, professionals are the most mobile category, as about 60 percent of them started work in a different category. In Hungary the category of white-collar workers is equally mobile, while in Poland, less than half (47 percent) started work in a different category.

The category of skilled workers (and, in Poland, white-collar workers as well) can be regarded as semi-mobile in both countries. (In Poland, every second, and in Hungary only every third, skilled worker started work in a different category.) The category of semi-skilled and unskilled workers is the most stable in both countries. In Hungary 80 percent, and in Poland 71 percent, started work as unskilled workers. The effect of the structural differences in agriculture are seen at their most direct in this category. In Hungary every fifth industrial unskilled or semi-skilled worker started work in agriculture as an unskilled worker, while in Poland the figure is one in ten. As the proportion of people who started work as individual farmers in agriculture is insignificant in both countries (1-2 percent), this difference is connected primarily with the technical development of large-scale agriculture in Hungary, which enabled the flow of a significant proportion of unskilled agricultural workers into industry.

Restratification through exchange of occupation with regard to category, is different in both countries. Thirteen percent of unskilled and semi-skilled workers employed in industry in Hungary, and 22 percent in Poland, started work as skilled workers. We do not know the reason for this 'downgrading', but presumably skilled jobs that were badly paid or particularly difficult, and the so-called 'disappearing' trades, were exchanged for unskilled or semi-skilled jobs. The relatively high rate in Poland is also connected with the different method of sampling.

The proportion of people who exchanged professional jobs for unskilled or semi-skilled jobs is insignificant in both countries (2-3 percent); there is therefore practically no flow from professional careers into unskilled manual fields in either country.[4]

In Hungary, similarly, there is no flow from the field of white-collar work to skilled jobs, while in Poland 7 percent of skilled workers started work as white-collar workers. In Poland the percentage of skilled workers who started work as unskilled or semi-skilled workers and later acquired qualifications is higher than in Hungary (Poland 40 percent, Hungary 33 percent).

In Hungary more than half of the white-collar workers started as manual workers (Hungary 56 percent, Poland 42 percent). In both countries 50 percent of these started as unskilled or semi-skilled and 50 percent as skilled workers. A proportion of the workers in both countries, particularly women, find the white-collar clerical jobs, involving ‘sitting at a desk’, more attractive.

A much greater proportion of professional people started work as manual workers in Hungary (36 percent) than in Poland (23 percent). Furthermore, while the proportions of unskilled and skilled workers that moved into the professional category are equal in Hungary, in Poland the proportion of professionals who were formerly skilled workers (15 percent) is double the percentage that started as unskilled workers (8 percent).[5]

Accordingly, more professionals in Poland (55 percent) started work in white-collar jobs (as clerical employees) than in Hungary (22 percent). There are more people in professional jobs in Hungary who started work as manual workers, which indicates that the percentages of so-called ‘promoted cadres’ is higher in Hungary than in Poland. Naturally there are also several workers-turned-professionals who acquired higher education and qualifications while working (see Table 1).

The concepts of ‘up’ and ‘down’ require clarification. It is obvious that, on the basis of the majority of society’s hierarchical principles, the professionals are on the highest, and unskilled manual workers on the lowest, level of the social hierarchies (e.g., power, knowledge, prestige and other hierarchies). Upward mobility represents movement from the manual to the non-manual category, from the unskilled to the skilled in the non-manual category, and from white-collar to professional work in the non-manual category. This main trend in mobility is clearly indicated by the data provided in the section on inter-generational and intra-generational mobility. Therefore, from the point of view of mobility paths, the hierarchy of categories can be regarded as stages in this movement from the unskilled manual jobs to professional jobs.

The ratio of respondents remaining in the same category (on the basis of original and present occupation) is higher for the manual category in Hungary than in Poland. In the professional category, and effectively in the white-collar category, the absence of mobility is identical in both countries.

Upward mobility is higher among skilled workers in Poland and

TABLE 1
Breakdown of Respondents, According to their First Socio-occupational Category in Hungary and Poland

First social category of respondent	Present social category of respondent: Unskilled or semi-skilled	Skilled workers	White-collar workers	Professional
	%	%	%	%
Unskilled or semi-skilled workers				
Hungary	80	32	27	17
Poland	71	40	21	8
Skilled workers				
Hungary	13	64	29	19
Poland	22	49	21	15
White-collar workers				
Hungary	2	1	41	22
Poland	3	7	53	35
Professionals				
Hungary	—	1	1	42
Poland	—	—	3	41
Farmers				
Hungary	2	—	1	—
Poland	1	—	—	—
Others				
Hungary	3	2	1	—
Poland	3	4	2	1
Total	100	100	100	100

among white-collar workers in Hungary; the ratio of downward mobility is higher among unskilled and semi-skilled workers in Poland than in Hungary; and there is hardly any downward mobility among the white-collar or skilled workers (see Table 2).

The intra-generational mobility of men and women differs considerably among the professionals. More than half the women and only one-third of the men started work in their present category. The difference between the original and present category is somewhat higher in Poland than in Hungary. There are many more men among professionals who started work as manual or white-collar workers than there are women. The difference between the mobility of men and women in the two categories of manual work is negligible. The intra-generational mobility among unskilled and semi-skilled workers is independent of age in both countries. In every age group there is a high ratio of workers who were originally unskilled or semi-skilled. In both countries there is a tendency for upward mobility to decrease with age, although this tendency was observed among the skilled to a lesser extent. In Hungary 70 percent, and in Poland 55 percent, of the 26-30-year-old group in the professional category started work as professionals, while the ratio of people over 50 who started work as professionals is not higher than 20 percent in either country. This tendency does not appear in white-collar jobs.

TABLE 2
The Trends of Intra-generational Mobility in Hungary and Poland, According to Socio-occupational Category

	Present occupation of respondent			
Present occupation compared with original*	**Profess-ionals**	**White-collar workers**	**Skilled workers**	**Unskilled or semi-skilled workers**
	%	%	%	%
Upwardly mobile				
Hungary	58	27	32	—
Poland	59	21	40	—
No change in level				
Hungary	42	72	67	85
Poland	41	76	60	75
Downwardly mobile				
Hungary	—	1	1	15
Poland	—	3	—	25

*Based on the following levels:
Top level — professionals
bottom level — unskilled manual
medium level — all other social categories.

The size of the residential area is only weakly connected with intra-generational mobility, and the trends are different in the two countries. The mobility of unskilled workers is independent of the size of residential area. In Hungary the proportion of white-collar workers and professionals who were formerly manual workers — and of professionals who were formerly white-collar workers — is somewhat higher in the countryside. In Poland the ratio of those who came from another category into their present category is lowest in the villages. This tendency holds for all categories except that of the unskilled and semi-skilled.

INTER-GENERATIONAL MOBILITY

In the long term, the difference in the development of agriculture in both countries caused a significant difference in the data on inter-generational mobility. In Poland, before the Second World War the percentage of agricultural workers was higher than in Hungary.[6] At the end of the 1940s the proportion of Polish agricultural workers started to approach the Hungarian figure. This was because of the 'disconnection' of the eastern Polish agricultural areas and the 'reconnection' of the industrialized western areas. Later, during the period of industrialization, the percentage of agricultural workers decreased in both countries. The decrease in Hungary was greater, however, because of the collectivization of agriculture. According to 1973/74 surveys the proportion of agricultural workers was 23.3 percent in Hungary and 34.7 percent in Poland. The difference thus not only reappeared but also increased.[7]

It is of interest that, despite considerable social restratification following the collectivization of agriculture in Hungary, there is a higher proportion of people in Hungary than in Poland who belong to the same socio-occupational category as their fathers (with the exception of the white-collar category). The proportion of immobiles is mainly higher among unskilled workers and professionals in Hungary, while the other two categories are roughly similar. This shows that, in terms of background influences, the lower and the upper categories in Hungary are somewhat more closed than in Poland (Table 3).

The reproduction of occupational status is thus of importance in the top and bottom categories. In the bottom category the lack of prospects and the impossibility of promotion meet with social disapprobation, while in the top category an advantageous position is monopolized. With regard to the amount of freezing of these two end categories, the situation in Poland seems to be more favourable (see Table 4).

TABLE 3
Respondents with Fathers in Independent and Non-independent Agricultural Occupations (Percentage per socio-occupational category)

Respondents	Hungary Inde-pendent	Hungary Non-in-dependent	Hungary Total	Poland Inde-pendent	Poland Non-in-dependent	Poland Total
	%	%	%	%	%	%
Unskilled or semi-skilled workers	13	24	37	28	10	38
Skilled workers	9	19	28	16	8	24
White-collar workers	5	12	17	18	4	22
Professionals	2	6	8	15	4	19

TABLE 4
Percentage of Respondents Belonging to Same Social Category as Father

	Hungary	Poland
	%	%
Unskilled or semi-skilled workers	65	55
Skilled workers	40	36
White-collar workers	8	12
Professionals	32	24

In both countries, with the exception of the professional category, the proportion of industrial workers whose father was an agricultural worker developed similarly under the impact of a similar form of industrialization. However, there is a considerable difference in the percentage of workers originating from independent farmers,[8] which is linked to the fact that small farming preserved its dominant role in Polish agriculture (Table 5).

TABLE 5
Breakdown of Respondents, According to their Father's Occupation in Hungary and Poland

Father's occupation	Present occupation of respondents: Unskilled or semi-skilled workers	Skilled workers	White-collar workers	Professionals
	%	%	%	%
Individual farmers				
Hungary	13	9	5	2
Poland	28	16	18	15
Unskilled or semi-skilled workers				
Hungary	52	42	33	17
Poland	27	26	21	9
Skilled workers				
Hungary	24	37	39	32
Poland	33	38	31	27
White-collar workers				
Hungary	2	3	8	13
Poland	5	9	14	16
Professionals				
Hungary	3	4	10	32
Poland	3	7	12	24
Merchants, craftsmen				
Hungary	6	5	5	4
Poland	4	4	4	9
Total	100	100	100	100

The number of professionals considerably decreased in Poland during the Second World War. This may have been because of the dissolution of some of the professional families or because of a transfer into another category. As a result, the proportion of professionals with professional fathers is much lower in Poland than in Hungary. However, the percentage of people with a professional background is higher in Poland than in Hungary in all other categories (Table 6).

TABLE 6
Percentage of Respondents who have Professional Origins*

	Hungary	Poland
Unskilled or semi-skilled workers		
Skilled workers	4	7
White-collar workers	10	12
Professionals	32	24

* Measured by occupation of father.

In Hungary nine-tenths of the respondents in the two manual categories reported that their father was also a manual worker. In Poland the proportion was a little lower: 88 percent of the unskilled and semi-skilled had a manual worker father and 86 percent of the skilled workers. In Hungary 80 percent of the white-collar workers and 50 percent of the professionals had a father who was a manual worker. In Poland the 'jump' is smaller — the percentage of professionals with a manual worker father is somewhat over 50 percent. The proportion of manual worker fathers decreases in each socio-occupational category if unskilled workers are taken to the bottom level and professionals on the top and an upward line is drawn. (Table 7). The division of men and women according to background among manual workers hardly differs in Hungary and differs not at all in Poland.

TABLE 7
Percentage of Workers with a Manual Background (including independent farmers)

	Hungary	**Poland**
	%	%
Unskilled or semi-skilled workers	89	88
Skilled workers	88	80
White-collar workers	77	70
Professionals	51	51

The composition of professionals according to background varies markedly according to sex in both countries. There is a higher ratio of professional men with an unskilled worker father, and the proportion of professional women with a professional father is higher than for professional men.

TABLE 8
Directions of Mobility (inter-generational) Compared with the Occupation of the Father in Hungary and Poland per Socio-occupational Category*

Present occupation of respondent compared with father	Present occupation of respondent			
	Profess-ionals	White-collar workers	Skilled workers	Unskilled or semi-skilled workers
	%	%	%	%
Upward mobility				
Hungary	68	38	51	—
Poland	76	39	43	—
Immobile				
Hungary	32	8	37	53
Poland	24	14	38	27
Downward mobility				
Hungary	—	10	4	35
Poland	—	12	7	45
Mobile on the same level or unclassifiable				
Hungary	3	44	8	13**
Poland	7	35	13	28**
Total	100	100	100	100

*Calculated according to the following levels:
top level — professionals
bottom level — unskilled workers
medium level — other social categories.

**These 13 percent in Hungary and 28 percent in Poland of unskilled or semi-skilled workers had independent farmer fathers. These respondents cannot be classified from the point of direction.

The extent and direction of inter-generational mobility compared with the occupation of the father is category-specific. There is a relatively small difference between the same categories according to country, while there are significant differences between the categories themselves. Where upward mobility is concerned, two-thirds of the professionals in Hungary, and three-quarters in Poland; 40-50 percent of the skilled workers, and about one-third of the white-collar workers are higher in the hierarchy than their fathers. Differences in the rates of downward mobility in Poland and Hungary — taking into account the higher absolute value for Poland — can primarily be found among skilled workers. In Hungary 35 percent of the unskilled workers, and in Poland 45 percent had a father placed above them on the hierarchy. Within the two middle categories the ratio of downward mobility is also higher in Poland, but the difference is insignificant (see Table 8).

MOBILITY PATHS

In our examination of mobility routes, instead of the former three groups, in which skilled workers and white-collar workers were placed on the same level, we worked with four socio-occupational categories. In our survey the category of white-collar workers was placed higher in the hierarchy than the category of skilled workers. This was not a type of value judgement, but a difference from the point of view of mobility, which classifies the group according to the main trend in the direction of social mobility.

Our definition of mobility types was based on a consideration of the respondent's father's occupation and the first and present occupation of respondent. On this basis 29 percent of all respondents in Poland, and 34 percent in Hungary, belonged to the same socio-occupational category as the father, and their present and first job were also the same. The highest ratio of immobiles was found in both countries among the unskilled and semi-skilled workers (in Poland 41 percent; in Hungary 55 percent) (see Table 9).

'Dynasties' are therefore the most frequent in this category.[9] In Poland the 'dynastic' nature of skilled workers is relatively low (19 percent) among those in industry, but it is a little higher in Hungary (28 percent). Thus where skilled workers are concerned, either the respondent did not start as a skilled worker or the respondent's father was not a skilled worker.

In both countries, the ratio of immobiles was lowest among white-collar workers (6-9 percent), i.e., workers who started work as white-collar workers and whose fathers were in the same category.

TABLE 9
Breakdown of Respondents, According to Father's Occupation in Hungary and Poland

Father's occupation	Present occupation of respondent: Unskilled or semi-skilled workers	Skilled workers	White-collar workers	Professional
	%	%	%	%
Agricultural individual farmers				
Hungary	13	9	5	2
Poland	28	16	18	15
Unskilled or semi-skilled workers				
Hungary	52	42	33	17
Poland	27	26	21	9
Skilled workers				
Hungary	24	37	39	32
Poland	33	38	31	27
White-collar workers				
Hungary	2	3	8	13
Poland	5	9	14	16
Professionals				
Hungary	3	4	10	32
Poland	3	7	12	24
Merchants, craftsmen				
Hungary	6	5	5	4
Poland	4	4	4	9
Total	100	100	100	100

The related data on professionals differ in the two countries. In Poland 8 percent and in Hungary 19 percent of professionals started work in and had fathers in the same socio-occupational category. The proportion of professionals whose father was a professional but who started work as unskilled workers was 6 percent in Hungary and 8 percent in Poland. As we considered the first occupation to have been a result of some compulsion, we combined these data. Therefore, in Hungary the 'dynastic rate' among professionals engaged in industry is 25 percent and 16 percent in Poland. These ratios come close to those of skilled workers in both countries.

The analysis of the actual mobility paths was rather difficult, because in order to obtain clear categories (apart from stagnation or immobility) we had to distinguish eight different routes, relating to mobility and direction of an inter- or intra-generational nature. The types of mobility routes, illustrated by the relevant data, are shown in Table 10.

TABLE 10
Mobility Routes*

	Percentage of respondents	
	Hungary	**Poland**
Gradually down	1	2
Only intermobile down	12	17
Only intramobile down	2	6
Returning** with an upward detour	4	8
Immobile	34	29
Returning** with a downward detour	9	7
Only intramobile up	13	9
Only intermobile up	16	10
Gradually up	4	2
Unknown	5	10
Total	100	100

*This concerns the mobility route from the occupation of the father to the present occupation of respondent via first occupation.
**The term 'returning' means that, on the basis of first occupation, the respondent belonged to a different occupational category from his or her father, but on the basis of present occupation belongs to the same category.

Because of the relatively low number of respondents in the various categories, the data in the table cannot be analysed in detail. However, if we disregard the direction of mobility, then the data from the two countries can be compared with regard to the amount of mobility. We find that they are practically identical. If we reduce the data of the previous table, the proportion of inter-generational mobiles (whose original and present occupation is similar, while different from that of the father) is 27-28 percent. In both countries the ratio of intra-generational mobiles (first occupation is similar to that of the father, but present occupation is different) is 15 percent. The ratio of inter-and intra-generational mobiles is 18-19 percent and within this, the 'restitutive' mobility (i.e. where the first occupation differs from the category of the father's, while the present one returns to it) is 13 percent in Hungary and 15 percent in Poland.

Several macroscopic generalizations can be derived from the data about comparative developments in the two countries. Single-step mobility (either inter- or intra-generational) is characteristic mainly of skilled and white-collar workers in both countries. The mobile members of the unskilled and semi-skilled, white-collar and professional categories are characterized by the fact that the inter-generational mobiles are in the majority; that is, most workers started work in their present category. There is a much lower ratio of workers who started work in the same category as the father and later changed course. A differing tendency appears in the two countries with regard to the upward mobility of the two middle categories. In Hungary inter-generational mobility is higher than intra-generational mobility among the skilled workers' group and in Poland this is the case for the white-collar group.

Double-step mobility (both inter- and intra-generational) is a climb up the hierarchy when the movement is consistently from the unskilled to the white-collar and professional group. However, 'restitutive' mobility has to be taken into consideration when two steps are involved: in Poland it is higher among skilled workers than white-collar workers; in Hungary it is similar for both groups. In Hungary 8 percent, and in Poland 11 percent, of the unskilled and semi-skilled workers tried to 'break away' from their situation with their first occupation, but then relapsed. In Hungary 1 percent and in Poland 6 percent of these unsuccessful attempts to rise were made among the skilled workers.

With regard to upward mobility, similar tendencies can be found in both countries according to sex. Both double-step and intra-generational upward mobility are more frequent among males and inter-generational among females. In both countries there is a larger percentage of unsuccessful attempts to rise among women. In Poland the frequency of downward mobility is roughly identical in the case of men and women, while in Hungary inter-generational downward mobility is higher among women (15 percent) than among males (10 percent).

According to the first year of employment, the ratio of inter-generational mobility is similar in both countries. It is lower in the older age groups and higher in the younger age groups. The difference between the two is about fivefold, but the ratios in Hungary consistently surpass those of Poland.

THE SOCIO-OCCUPATIONAL STRUCTURE OF THE FAMILY

In Hungary, if the occupation of the spouse and wage-earning children is taken into consideration, the proportion of homogeneous families, according to socio-occupational category, is about 10-12 percent among manual workers, 9 percent among professionals and about 2 percent among white-collar workers. In Poland the percentages are lower (unskilled and semi-skilled workers 8 percent, skilled workers 4 percent, white-collar workers 3 percent and professionals 4 percent).

In both countries, the percentages of homogeneous families, of those who 'tend' upward or downward, and of those whose members belong to different categories, as some of them have shifted over time, are roughly the same in both countries.[10] However, in Hungary there is a larger ratio of respondents whose present occupation is higher than the original occupation, and higher than the occupations of other members of the family. Cases where the respondent's present occupation is the lowest in the family (where the respondent is downwardly mobile and the spouse and wage-earning child are in a higher category) are more frequent in Poland than in Hungary (see Table 11).

In Hungary the upward-'tending' family composition (when the first occupation of father and respondent is not higher, and occupation of spouse and child is not lower, than the present occupation of respondent) is most frequent among skilled workers (42 percent), followed by white-collar workers (32 percent), professionals (29 percent), and unskilled and semi-skilled workers

(26 percent). In Poland the corresponding percentages are 48-50 percent for skilled workers, white-collar workers and professionals, and 25 percent for unskilled and semi-skilled workers. In both countries downward-'tending' composition increases with the social hierarchy. The family structure that can be described as one where the respondent is on 'top' (when the respondent has moved upwards but family members have not) is most frequent among professionals in both countries. In Hungary 55 percent and in Poland 41 percent of professional respondents were in this category. Equivalent figures for white-collar workers are lower in Hungary (52 percent) but much lower in Poland (30 percent).

TABLE 11
Breakdown of Respondents According to Family Structure, Defined by Four or Five Occupations, in Hungary and Poland*

Mobility routes	Hungary	Poland
	%	%
Upward tendency	33	35
Downward tendency	12	10
Respondent in top position	23	10
Respondent in bottom position	10	24
Changing between categories	9	11
Intra-category stagnation	13	10
Total	100	100

*Based on married respondents according to following occupations:
1. father's occupation
2. first occupation of respondent
3. present occupation of respondent
4. occupation of respondent's spouse
5. occupation of wage-earning child (if any).

In Hungary families in which the respondent has the lowest position (when family members of the 'demoted' respondent belong to a higher socio-occupational category) were 25 percent among unskilled workers, 2 percent among skilled workers and 1 percent among white-collar workers. Such a type of family composition in Poland occurred among 37 percent of unskilled workers, 9 percent of skilled workers and 3 percent of white-collar workers.

In both countries the 'respondent on top' pattern was more frequent among men. This means, perhaps, that ambition is greater among men and that there are more men than women who cannot transmit their achieved level to their close kin. In both countries there are more women than men in lower-status jobs than their fathers (and perhaps lower than their first occupation), but whose spouse and children occupy a higher level.

To ascertain how far the socio-occupational categories are open or closed, in addition to the examination of mobility, a comparison of the occupation of spouse and friends with that of the respondent was undertaken.[11]

SPOUSES

In Hungary the ratio of spouses belonging to the same socio-occupational category is higher among manual workers whereas in Poland it is higher among professionals. The difference between the two countries is the greatest at the extremes: the unskilled and semi-skilled workers and the professionals. In Poland the spouses of 21 percent of unskilled and semi-skilled workers are also unskilled and semi-skilled workers, compared with 38 percent for Hungary. In Poland 53 percent of married professionals have professional spouses, while in Hungary the ratio is 39 percent.

The ratio of unqualified spouses (including independent farmers[12] and housewives) is almost identical: half of the unskilled and semi-skilled workers, one-third of the skilled workers, one-sixth of the white-collar workers, and one-tenth of the professionals have unqualified spouses.

In Hungary the ratio of skilled worker spouses is higher in every category than in Poland, and the biggest difference is in the category of white-collar workers: 37 percent of Hungary's white-collar workers, compared with 24 percent in Poland, have a skilled worker spouse.

In Poland the ratio of professional spouses among unskilled workers (17 percent) and skilled workers (34 percent) is almost double that of Hungary (9 and 19 percent respectively). We can therefore conclude that, in Poland, marriage into the manual categories is more open than in Hungary. However, when the proportion of skilled workers among the spouses of professionals is considered, the difference is in the opposite direction in the two countries: the professional category is more closed in Poland.

Mobility surveys show that mobility through marriage is different for men and women. There are more white-collar, unskilled or semi-skilled workers among the wives of manual and white-collar workers than among the husbands of manual and white-collar workers. Thus, a larger proportion of husbands than wives are skilled workers in every category — wives work at lower levels of both manual and non-manual work. Among the professionals, professional women marry professional men more often than vice versa. Marriage with persons placed higher in the social hierarchy (upward marriage mobility) is more frequent among women in every category in both countries.[13] As the situation of the family (and thus the wife) is defined by the position of the husband in the social hierarchy, marriage is a means of mobility for women, in addition to occupational change on their own part.

The data on the two countries show that such tendencies are sometimes more powerful in Hungary. However, there is a somewhat different tendency in the two middle categories. In both countries about three-quarters of the unskilled and semi-skilled women are married to men on a higher grade of the social hierarchy. In Poland, however, two-thirds of unskilled and semi-skilled men, and in Hungary one-third of the unskilled and semi-skilled men, are married to skilled workers or professionals.

In Poland almost the same percentage of skilled male workers (35 percent) is married to white-collar wives as white-collar women are married to skilled worker husbands (34 percent). Therefore marriage among the members of the two middle categories occurs with the same frequency with regard to sex.

However, in Hungary only 20 percent of skilled male workers are married to white-collar wives, while half the white-collar women are married to skilled worker husbands (Table 12).

FRIENDS

In line with marital relations, friendship is more open among the manual categories in Poland and among the professionals in

TABLE 12
Breakdown of Married Respondents, According to Upward or Downward Mobility through Marriage, per Sex and per Category, in Hungary and Poland

		Present occupation of respondent			
Present occupation of spouse compared with that of respondent*		Profess-ionals	White-collar workers	Skilled workers	Unskilled or semi-skilled workers
		%	%	%	%
Upward-tending					
Hungary:	men	—	10	4	34
	women		23	7	71
Poland:	men	—	18	13	66
	women	—	27	13	77
Homogeneous					
Hungary:	men	30	52	43	66
	women	75	19	73	29
Poland:	men	51	56	34	34
	women	80	36	58	23
Identical level but not homogeneous					
		—	20	20	—
	women	—	52	7	—
Poland:	men	—	23	35	—
	women	—	34	21	—
Downward-tending					
Hungary:	men	70	18	33	—
	women	25	6	13	—
Poland:	men	49	3	18	—
	women	20	3	8	—
Total		100	100	100	100

*We consider the case to be upward-tending when the spouse of the respondent is placed on a higher level in the following occupation hierarchy:

top level — professional
medium level — skilled worker and white-collar worker
bottom level — unskilled and semi-skilled worker.

Hungary. In Hungary the proportion of professionals who make friends in their own category is 69 percent and in Poland 78 percent, while the ratio of white-collar workers with white-collar friends is 29 percent in Hungary and 36 percent in Poland. In Hungary two-thirds of the skilled workers, and in Poland less than a half of the skilled workers, make friends within their own category. The ratio of unskilled and semi-skilled workers who make friends within their own category is 38 percent in Hungary and 16 percent in Poland.

During earlier surveys, we found an upward trend in relations of friendship among Hungarian non-manual workers, but because we worked only with non-manual samples, the full hierarchy was not scrutinized. According to the data of our present survey, the 'upward tendency' in making friends is present throughout the entire social hierarchy. This tendency is most powerful among the unskilled and semi-skilled workers, with white-collar workers second, in both countries. However, it is relatively weak among skilled workers. The extent of the upward tendency in making friends is about twice as strong in all the three categories in Poland than in Hungary. In Poland 65 percent of the unskilled and semi-skilled workers (Hungary 38 percent), 40 percent of the white-collar workers (Hungary 22 percent) and 15 percent of the skilled workers (Hungary 6 percent) named those whose occupation was higher than their own as their best friend.

As the survey of Hungarian non-manual workers showed,[14] the ratio of a social group who made friends with people on a higher social level is not counterbalanced by a comparable number of the higher-level group making friends with those from lower levels.

Most of the respondents had several friends on various levels of the social hierarchy, but the majority of people considered their friend with the highest status to be their best friend. It cannot, therefore, be concluded that such relations are mutual (see Table 13).

The friendship relationships of men and women differ significantly in Hungary. Conservative features in the situation of Hungarian women are indicated by the following facts. While only about one-tenth of the men have no friend, one-third or one-quarter of female manual and white-collar workers, and 14 percent of professional women, have no friend. In Poland, 16-20 percent of the unskilled and semi-skilled workers, 11 percent of the white-collar and skilled workers and 8 percent of the professionals have

TABLE 13
Breakdown of Respondents, According to Direction of Friendship Relations, per Category, in Hungary and Poland

Direction	Present occupation of respondent			
	Profes-sionals	White-collar workers	Skilled workers	Unskilled or semi-skilled workers
	%	%	%	%
Upward-tending				
Hungary	—	22	6	38
Poland	—	40	15	65
Intra-category friendship				
Hungary	69	29	65	38
Poland	78	36	46	16
Friendly with members of another category at same level				
Hungary	—	24	5	—
Poland	—	12	18	—
Downward-tending				
Hungary	21	3	7	—
Poland	14	2	9	—
No friends				
Hungary	10	22	17	24
Poland	8	10	12	19
Total	100	100	100	100

*See footnote to Table 12 (data on marital relations)

no friend, but the percentage hardly varies according to sex. In Hungary a smaller proportion of male white-collar workers (23 percent) make friends within their own category than do women white-collar workers (48 percent), and a larger ratio (40 percent) make friends with professionals than do women (19 percent). Consequently, Hungarian female white-collar workers have more friends among skilled workers and male white-collar workers have more friends among professionals.

COMPARISON OF MARITAL RELATIONS AND FRIENDSHIP RELATIONS IN CONNECTION WITH OCCUPATIONAL POSITIONS

The comparison of marital relations and friendship relations produced interesting and different results in both countries. With regard to Polish women, friendship relations are very like marital relations among manual workers. The percentage of marriage and friendships within the occupational category and the proportions of women married and befriended by members of the same category is, for example, almost identical among unskilled and semi-skilled workers and is very similar among skilled workers. However, the data on marital relations and friendship in Poland with regard to white-collar workers are different. One-third of female white-collar workers have a skilled worker husband, but only one-tenth of them make friends with skilled workers. Here, friendship within the same category is much higher than marriage within it. Conversely while only 27 percent of Polish female white-collar workers are married to professionals, 40 percent make friends with professionals. The ratio of professional women (11 percent) who make friends with members of other categories is again lower than the marital ratio (20 percent).

The data on the Hungarian professional women were almost identical to those for the Polish professional women, but there was some difference in inter-category marital proportions. More Hungarian professional women (16 percent) have skilled worker husbands than Polish (4 percent). Professional women have a single-step upward tendency, as 18 percent have white-collar friends but only 7 percent are married to white-collar workers. Relations of friendship between professionals and white-collar workers are less numerous than marital relations (6 and 16 percent respectively). There is a similar tendency among Hungarian female white-collar workers, but in contrast to Poland friendship with professionals is lower than marital relations with them.

The Hungarian structure of marital relations and friendship with regard to female skilled workers is almost identical to that of Poland. However, there is an opposite tendency among unskilled and semi-skilled female workers. The unskilled and semi-skilled female workers who are friendly with professionals are less numerous than the female workers who are married to professionals. There are more marital relations between unskilled and semi-skilled female workers and skilled workers (60 percent) than relations of friendship (35 percent). The ratio of unskilled and semi-skilled female workers who are married to unskilled and semi-skilled workers is 29 percent, but the proportion of friends chosen from the same category is much higher (50 percent). The group of Hungarian unskilled and semi-skilled female workers is the only group in the two countries where the upward tendency in making friends does not surpass that of their marital relations.

A comparison of the patterns of male marriage and friendship shows that these two types of social relations are different from corresponding female patterns. The same tendencies dominate in each category in the two countries, but they are more pronounced in Hungary than in Poland. From the unskilled and semi-skilled up to the professionals, the amount of social distinction between wives and friends increased hierarchically among the male respondents of both countries: there are more friends than wives in a higher socio-occupational category.

In Hungary unskilled and semi-skilled male workers have fewer friends than wives in their own category, and are orientated primarily towards skilled workers in their friendships. However, in Poland unskilled and semi-skilled workers also look for friends among professionals.

In both countries, skilled male workers keep their friendship relations — more than their marital relations — within their own socio-occupational category. Friendships with unskilled and semi-skilled workers, or with white-collar workers, are less common than marital relations with them — 45 percent of Hungarian skilled workers have a skilled worker wife but 79 percent have a skilled worker friend.[15]

In the choice of friends, particularly in Hungary, there is a distinction between manual and non-manual workers and men tend to determine friendship patterns in the manual categories. Manual workers have almost no friends among professionals, while white-collar workers have a considerable number (40-50 percent). This distinction can also be found, to a lesser extent, among women. The determinant role of men in the choice of friends is illustrated by the fact that a large proportion of male manual workers have no friends among white-collar workers although some of them have white-collar wives.

Among couples at least one of which is a professional, there is an unambiguous orientation in friendship towards professionals, which is independent of whether it is the husband or the wife who is the person in the professional job.

The two types of social relations under discussion can be considered important from the point of view of the individual. They belong to the private sphere and are freely chosen. As both relations have emotional implications, we feel that their joint analysis and comparison is justified. It seemed appropriate to examine them independently of any connection they might have to collectives, place of work and other social groups, since these have a completely different nature as they belong to the community sphere and are less voluntary. As our comparative survey did not aim at a thorough analysis of marital relations and relations of friendship, we can only formulate hypotheses from the results gained.

The very conspicuous 'upward trend' in making friends may have several reasons behind it. It is a natural impulse to give and to receive such things as information, knowledge, advice, patterns of life, emotional support and financial assistance in social relations. These requirements and desires can usually be satisfied more fully through the help of people higher in the social hierarchy. We therefore consider the search for and maintenance of 'upward-tending' human relations to be understandable and justified. In addition to ambition and a healthy wish to rise in the social hierarchy, there may be motives involving 'substitutive' gratification and success by 'association'. It can be presumed that some people try to compensate for their dissatisfaction with their choice of spouse, or earlier unsatisfactory opportunities, through friends; or, instead of improving their work situation themselves, they may try to gain promotion through pulling strings. It is possible that some people (primarily in the provinces) look for a defence against the local bosses through friends in a higher position. All these suggestions, however, could only be affirmed after further research.

In sum, our surveys indicate that considerable social restratification occurred in both countries in the past decades. The extent of mobility — primarily because of the more frequent incidence of downward mobility — is higher in Poland than in Hungary. This is of interest because the Hungarian data embody the effects of the significant restratification following the collectivization of agriculture, which did not take place in Poland.

In both countries — at least among industrial workers — the extent of mobility has hardly reduced since then. A certain closure has taken place among professionals, with a corresponding reduction in their infiltration by other socio-occupational categories.

In both Poland and Hungary the most closed category is that of unskilled and semi-skilled workers, and it is more closed in Hungary than in Poland. In Hungary the professional category is more open than in Poland, and in Poland the other three categories are more open than in Hungary. The ratio of 'dynasties' is high (40-50 percent) among unskilled and semi-skilled workers. Among skilled workers, where 'dynasties' might be held desirable from the 'trade' point of view, the ratio is relatively low (20-30 percent). There are even fewer professional dynasties (15-25 percent), and almost none among white-collar workers (6-9 percent).

Women and young people are more inter-mobile, while men and elderly people are more intra-mobile. In Hungary there were more respondents in the 'top' position within the family structure, whereas in Poland the situation of the respondents was the reverse. In both countries respondents 'on the top' were primarily men and respondents 'on the bottom' were primarily women.

In Poland marital relations and relations of friendship are more open in the manual categories, and in Hungary they are more open in the professional category. In both countries wives frequently have jobs of a lower prestige than their husbands — they marry 'upward'.

The 'upward trend' in making friends is more powerful in Poland. In both countries the manual categories and the professionals are to some extent dichotomized in terms of friendship, and skilled workers make friends almost exclusively within their own category.

The analysis of the results of our survey brought to light several known and lesser known phenomena. The tendencies experienced in the two countries are very similar in many cases, and occasionally identical. As our survey aimed at a general comparison between the two countries, further research is necessary for a more detailed analysis.

NOTES

1. Upward mobility can be described as favourable because of the advantages accompanying the rise in social status. However, double-stage upward mobility frequently causes constant tension.

2. We recognize only what is termed 'status mobility'. However, numerous American sociologists consider the notion of 'prestige mobility' to be decisive.

3. According to some authors (e.g. S.M. Lipset, H. Zetterberg, R. Bendix, etc.) the amount of social mobility depends primarily on the level of economic development, and differences between modes of development have less influence. The results of the Hungarian-Polish comparison do not seem to contradict this. See for example S.M. Lipset and H. Zetterberg, *A Theory of Social Mobility*, London, International Sociological Association, 1956.

4. According to a few American surveys, there is more social mobility within occupational categories than between manual and non-manual workers. The movement from non-manuals to manuals (and inversely) occurs relatively rarely. In Hungary and Poland there is only the first type of movement — from non-manuals to manuals. See for example S.M. Lipset and R. Bendix, *Social Mobility in Industrial Society*, Berkeley and Los Angeles, University of California Press, 1962.

5. Most probably, there are many professionals who started as unskilled workers because they were not immediately admitted to university, and thus took temporary unskilled jobs. As our survey did not cover an examination of careers, we thus have no relevant data.

6. According to the 1930-31 census, 70.3 percent of wage-earners in Poland and 54.5 percent in Hungary were engaged in agriculture. See R. Andorka and K. Zagórski, *Social Mobility in Hungary and Poland — Statistical Booklet*, Budapest, Central Statistical Office, 1979, p. 11.

7. Ibid.

8. Fathers who were independent farmers have to be regarded as unskilled manual workers. Their ratio in Hungary was 13 percent and in Poland 26 percent. If the independent farmer fathers are excluded from Table 4, 52 percent of unskilled and semi-skilled workers in Hungary, and 27 percent in Poland, belong to the same socio-occupational category as their father.

9. The expression 'dynasty' is not fully justified, because we did not know the occupation of the grandfather. But we assumed that, if the respondent's first and present occupation corresponded to that of the father, there was a status inheritance, which is one step away from a 'dynasty'.

10. Chronology here means that the present occupation of the respondent was preceded by the first occupation and the father's occupation. The first occupation of the respondent and that of the father also preceded the occupation of spouse and children. Respondents were usually gainfully employed when they got married. The trend displayed in the composition of the family according to occupation is based on these notions.

11. In this section, the occupation of the respondent is compared with the occupation of spouse and best friend. The combined analysis is justified because both forms of relationships are of an emotional character, based on inter-personal

choice, can be dissolved and re-established with another person, etc.

12. A spouse who was an independent farmer occurred among only 2 percent of Polish unskilled workers.

13. Except, naturally, the professionals, because female professionals cannot find higher-placed husbands. However, there are more professional husbands in leading positions than wives.

14. See for example György Akszentievics, 'Social Relations of Provincial Intellectuals', in *The Situation of Provincial Intellectuals*, Vol. 3: *Social Relations of the Intellectuals in Budapest* (manuscript), 1971.

15. This is also the result of the higher number of skilled male workers than skilled female workers.

2

WORK CONDITIONS AND ACTIVITIES

Maria Jarosińska

There are technological, organizational, economic and human factors in the process of production that takes place in industrial units of a complex structure. The basis of industrial production is the equipment required for the manufacturing of a given product, to which the organizational order, with its principles of division of competence and hierarchy, is partly subordinated. The human factor conforms to such principles. Basic differentiations in a community of workers arise when such factors occupy different positions. Such differences caused by the division of labour include the type and content of work, qualifications, and the conditions under which work is performed. More indirect causes of differentiation include extra pay and chances for promotion. Both direct and indirect differentiation bring about different behaviour among workers, as well as different attitudes, expectations, motives and values, which are either established by the division of labour or are a reaction to it.

The large number of factors and principles at work in the complex industrial structure of today results in their intersection. There are factors and principles that neutralize each other and blur existing forms of differentiation, and others that overlap and deepen existing types of differentiation. Individual characteristics of a worker, such as age, sex, social background, education, needs and expectations, can either deepen or blur such differences.[1]

Seen from the viewpoint of complex technological and organizational structures, the human factor in industry — manpower — is a marshalled and manipulated element. However, the principles of the political system and of society in general, as well as the practices of management, view workers from two different perspectives; both see workers as an independent social power and as subject to the production process. Workers in a socialist country are joint managers in their enterprises. This duality of roles performed — as a subordinate worker and a joint manager — and the conflicts between the two roles are a significant feature of the present time in socialist countries.

CONTENT OF WORK

Our survey, like others in the past, such as *Automation and Industrial Workers*,[2] in which Hungary and Poland participated, covers relations between the type and content of work and workers' socioeconomic situation and attitudes.

Problems concerning the relations between aspects of work, the workers' place in society and system of values have been investigated in the USA,[3] and a comprehensive study of problems of work motivation and workers' activity in relation to content and type of work has been completed in the Soviet Union.[4] The relationship between the content of work and work culture has also been examined in Poland.[5]

The starting point of any research involves clarifying the concept of work which is defined as a set of demands to be fulfilled by a worker. The description of the demands is fairly simple if we have to cope with one occupation or a group of related occupations. However, it is a job for the distant future to design a universal system of measurement of the content of work embracing all existing occupations. Here, we will try to introduce such a form of measurement for four basic categories of industrial employees.

Our investigation was concerned mainly with the differences and similarities between social categories, with regard to the work they performed, their attitudes toward the necessary effort, their working conditions and future prospects. Three aspects of workers' participation in the social division of work will be discussed:

(1) the type of work selected, with regard to the amount of physical and mental effort involved;

(2) content of work, as determined by the worker's actual activity on the job;

(3) place occupied in the managerial structure of an industrial enterprise.

This analysis covers, first, the type of work done by the social categories selected, and, second, the differences in its intensity.

Data include descriptions of respondents' work-load and the requirements imposed by tasks conducted in conformity with such norms. Each of these requirements was estimated on a nine-point scale, in which 1 signifies zero intensity and 9 the maximum. For both Hungary and Poland, the arithmetic mean of points was calculated for the work-load prevailing in the social categories selected.

TABLE 1

Type of Work Measured According to the Physical and Mental Effort Required in Different Socio-occupational Categories (arithmetical means calculated using a 9-point scale)

Specification	Hungary				Poland			
	Unskilled workers	Skilled workers	White-collar workers	Profes-sionals	Unskilled workers	Skilled workers	White-collar workers	Profes-sionals
1. Level of physical effort required	5.07	5.17	2.22	2.00	5.51	5.22	2.78	2.25
2. Degree of monotony of physical effort	4.98	4.26	2.85	2.95	5.24	4.53	2.95	2.53
3. Degree of physical hardship of working conditions	5.01	5.28	2.65	2.51	5.63	5.39	3.06	2.95
Mental effort related to:								
4. Independent decision-making	2.95	4.76	5.45	6.91	4.11	5.17	6.12	7.13
5. Complexity of instructions involved	3.19	5.06	5.61	6.85	3.59	4.81	6.00	6.90
6. Complexity of information involved	2.48	4.50	5.19	6.71	3.04	4.06	5.73	6.91
7. Necessity of continuous improvement of professional qualifications	1.76	3.77	3.76	5.97	3.19	4.39	5.69	6.52
Average physical work-load	5.02	4.90	2.57	2.48	5.46	5.05	2.93	2.58
Average mental work-load	2.59	4.52	5.00	6.61	3.48	4.61	5.88	6.86
Average physical and mental work-load	3.63	4.68	3.96	4.84	4.33	4.79	4.62	5.02

In respect of physical effort (Table 1, points 1, 2 and 3), the work of manual workers is basically different from that of non-manual workers. In Hungary, as opposed to Poland, there is more physical effort required and harder physical working conditions among skilled workers than unskilled workers. In both countries, the main difference, which is considerable, occurs between manual and non-manual workers. In the unautomated production process, a large amount of physical effort is required from manual workers, and despite the technological development that has been achieved in both countries, physical effort is still a defining feature of work. Table 1 shows that work is accomplished under difficult conditions and accompanied by a great monotony of tasks with little variety in the intensity required, particularly among unskilled workers.

Compared with manual workers, non-manual workers perform their jobs in comfortable working conditions, and there is little monotony or physical effort. Hungary is rather better off in this respect than Poland. If we regard manual workers as the point of reference, non-manual workers are a privileged group with regard to the first two characteristics selected. Where little physical effort is involved this can also function as an element of privilege if the social valuation of hard physical effort is negative.

This basic differentiation between the characteristics of work, with regard to its physical features, is reflected in the average values of the total physical work-load assigned to manual and non-manual workers. In the categories investigated these values form a rising scale with a significant 2 point difference between skilled and white-collar workers. The average physical work-load of unskilled workers is twice as heavy as that of professionals.

There is also a great difference in mental effort required in various types of work (Table 1, points 4, 5, 6 and 7). In Hungary the mental effort required from unskilled workers amounts to very little, but increases significantly (by nearly 2 points) for skilled workers. The highest level of mental effort is found among professionals, while the mental effort of a white-collar worker is only a little higher than that of a skilled worker.

In Poland the mental effort required, expressed in arithmetical terms, represents a steady upward curve which corresponds to an increase in the level of education of the successive social categories — an average rise of about 1 point.

The particular mental requirements of specific jobs determine the average value of the mental load for different categories of workers. In Hungary the middle categories, i.e., skilled and white-collar workers, are the most similar in this respect, while the most significant difference occurs between the two categories of manual workers (about 2 points), and a little less (1.61 points) distinguishes white-collar workers from professionals. In Poland the average mental work-load increases by about 1 point in each successive category.

The comparison of average physical and mental work-loads among the social categories reveals the existence of three types of work. The first type is work where physical effort is the prevailing feature accompanied by a very light mental work-load, which is in complete contrast to professionals and white-collar workers, where mental effort is the prevailing feature of their work and only a very slight physical work-load is entailed. The third type is skilled work where both physical and mental effort is required with a slight predominance in the physical work-load (below 0.5 points).

The last item in Table 1 (i.e. the total average physical and mental work-load) indicates that the 9 point scale is bottom-heavy. In Hungary the majority fall between 3.5 and 4.8 points and in Poland between 4.3 and 5.0 points. Nevertheless, the intensity of effort hovers around a medium level as the two types of effort are complementary to each other. In both countries intensity of effort lessens in each social category from the heaviest-loaded professionals, skilled workers and white-collar workers down to the unskilled workers. The results obtained contradict the current opinion that unskilled work is harder than white-collar work.

(However, it should be noted that white-collar work included not only office workers, who carry out routine tasks in industry, but also the complex work of technicians in the industrial production process. It is possible that some of the divergences recorded were caused by the classification employed, i.e., the calculation of the average work-load of this as a single social category.)

Figures 1, 2 and 3 illustrate the distribution of indices of physical effort and selected indicators of mental effort in different socio-occupational categories. It transpires that in both countries there are substantial internal differences in these categories. For both categories of workers, Table 2 lists the proportions of respondents requiring hard physical effort and relatively little physical effort. The corresponding figures indicating the amount of mental effort required from manual workers, assessed in relation to the extent of independent decision-making involved, can be seen in Table 3.

The phenomenon of accumulated hardship is another important problem. The empirical findings show that there is a distinct relation between the amount of physical effort required and the degree of hardship that results from working conditions — Cramer's V, calculated for the whole samples, amounts to 0.49 in

FIGURE 1
Level of Required Physical Effort

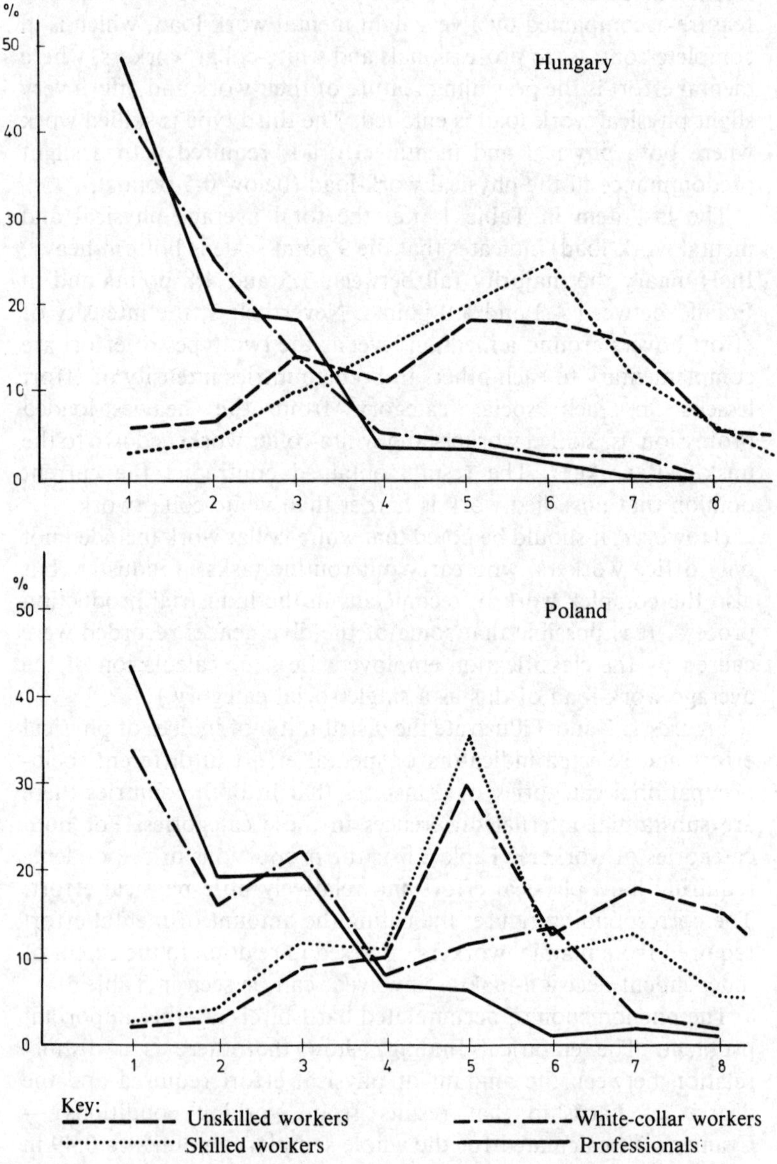

FIGURE 2
Mental Requirements: Independent Decision-making

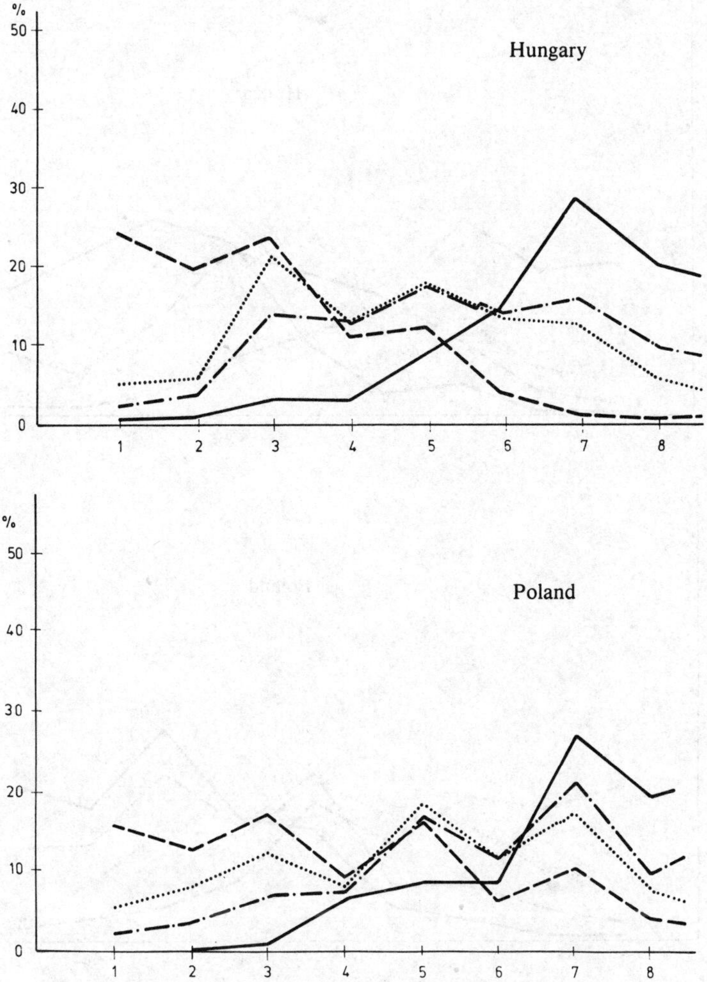

Key:
– – – – Unskilled workers
·········· Skilled workers
–·–·–·– White-collar workers
———— Professionals

FIGURE 3
Mental Requirements: Complexity of the Instructions Obtained

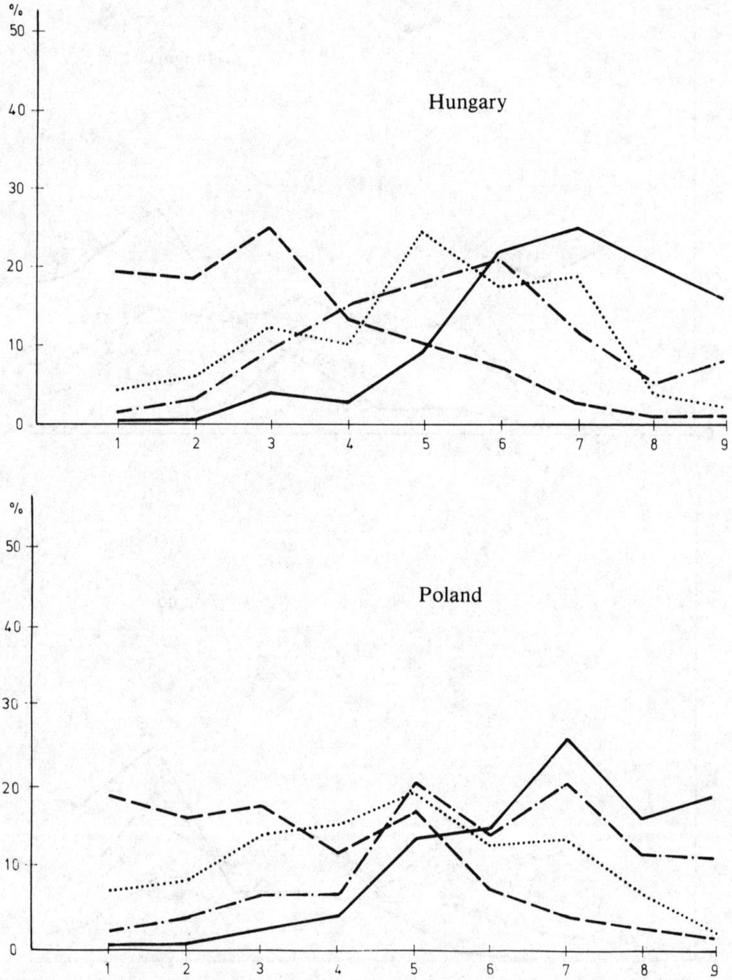

Key:
– – – – Unskilled workers — · — · — White-collar workers
·········· Skilled workers ———— Professionals

TABLE 2
Degree of Physical Effort Required

	Hungary		Poland	
	High	Low	High	Low
	%	%	%	%
Unskilled workers	27	26	39	15
Skilled workers	20	17	23	19

TABLE 3
Degree of Mental Effort Required

	Hungary		Poland	
	High	Low	High	Low
	%	%	%	%
Unskilled workers	3	69	19	46
Skilled workers	22	32	33	26

Hungary and 0.36 in Poland. In Hungary the proportion of unskilled workers whose work requires great physical efforts in conditions of hardship is 16 percent (Poland 23 percent), while the equivalent figures for skilled workers are 12 percent (Poland 16 percent). Such a situation does not occur among the professionals in the two countries and is sporadic among white-collar workers (Hungary 1 percent and Poland 2.4 percent).

As intense hardship of work affects a considerable proportion of manual workers, and only sporadically non-manual workers, the working conditions of white-collar workers and professionals appear to be privileged and those of manual workers to be the opposite. The fact that mental effort is cumulated among non-manual workers, and that it occurs to even higher degree than the cumulation characteristic of manual workers' physical efforts, is not socially equivalent. A great diversity of mental effort keeps up intellectual efficiency, while great physical effort in an environment of hardship results in the lessening of a worker's physical capability.

So far we have discussed the physical and mental effort that is necessary for fulfilling the different work tasks. The next problem, however, concerns workers' attitudes to the intensity of their work. It is measured by the importance attached by them to a lack of great physical and mental effort in work (Table 4).

TABLE 4
Importance Attached to Lack of Great Physical and Mental Effort in the Work of Different Social Categories (arithmetical means calculated using a 9-point scale)

Specification	Hungary				Poland			
	Unskilled workers	Skilled workers	White-collar workers	Profes-sionals	Unskilled workers	Skilled workers	White-collar workers	Profes-sionals
Great physical effort	6.78	6.41	5.96	4.98	6.39	6.51	5.40	5.14
Great mental effort	6.09	6.03	5.86	4.83	5.34	5.18	4.87	3.95

In all the social categories of both countries, the average importance attached to the release from great physical effort was larger than the importance attached to the release from mental effort. In both countries, the higher the probability of great physical effort, the greater the distaste. The average values attached to release from work involving great mental effort reveal the opposite tendency, as the higher the intensity of such efforts, the lower the average unwillingness to undertake it. Nevertheless, the differences between the unwillingness towards making physical effort and towards making mental effort are small — in Hungary 0.7 points and in Poland a little over 1 point. All the same, this difference in the figures for the two countries results in lower average values (indicative of a greater distaste for strenuous mental or physical effort) in each of the social categories for Poland, which is a possible indication of cultural differences existing between the two countries.

TABLE 5
Importance Attached to the Need to Utilize Different Kinds of Mental Effort in the Work of Different Social Categories (arithmetical means calculated using a 9-point scale)

Specification	Hungary				Poland			
	Unskilled workers	Skilled workers	White-collar workers	Profes-sionals	Unskilled workers	Skilled workers	White-collar workers	Profes-sionals
Need to make use of knowledge	5.40	7.03	7.13	7.86	5.98	7.08	7.51	8.09
Necessity of developing new techniques	4.94	6.51	6.58	7.22	4.43	5.77	6.13	7.22
Independence at work	6.18	7.39	7.64	7.96	5.51	6.49	7.13	7.78
Variety of tasks	5.70	6.87	7.32	7.84	5.56	6.77	7.02	7.67

These data should be compared directly with those concerning the importance attached to work the very nature of which requires mental effort. Positive values attached to mental effort are examined in Table 5.

In both countries the fact that average values fall towards the top of the scale signifies a very positive attitude among the respondents. Such features as the possibility of making use of knowledge, the necessity of developing new techniques, independence at work and the variety of work may, and sometimes must, require considerable mental effort. All of them are a confirmation of the worker's individual qualities and are essential elements in satisfying needs for self-realization and self-expression. It can therefore be supposed that the self-rewarding features of mental effort are the reason for its acceptance, and it is possible that such features offset the need to invest large amounts of mental effort at work. In both countries, the average values indicating a positive choice of work requiring considerable mental effort are higher than the average values indicating its rejection among skilled workers, white-collar workers and professionals. In Poland the same applies to unskilled workers, although it is possible that the data result from the composition of the sample. In Hungary unskilled workers only accord more points for independence at work, in comparison with a 'rejection score' for great mental effort.

Unskilled workers stand apart from the other categories because of the lowest level of acceptance given to mental aspects of work. In both countries the difference between unskilled and skilled workers is the largest (more than 2 points), whereas the other categories are relatively similar to each other.

A feature common to industrial workers in both countries, irrespective of social category, is a negative attitude towards physical effort, whch is a significant feature of the ethos of work. This effort is considered as an undesirable factor, especially as it is often accompanied by other hardships such as bad working conditions and little alteration in the required intensity. Negative attitudes towards great physical effort can be regarded as part of the industrial workers' system of values, despite the differentiating effect of the division of labour which requires such an effort from manual workers.

Social evaluation of the mental effort required is not unequivocal. If it is only an abstract element in the job, then its evaluation by the two categories of manual workers is quite strongly negative, but less negative on the part of non-manual workers.

The intensity of positive valuation increases when, owing to the particular features of work, a worker can confirm his or her individual capacities in it. The greater the saturation of a given group of jobs with an intellectual element, the higher its acceptance score. The requirements of the mental division of labour are clearly shown by the different scores reflecting rejection and acceptance of mental effort.

An analysis of a more detailed grouping of workers, categorized by the content of work is of interest. We grouped occupations according to the main tasks involved in them — a classification based on estimates of the duration of dominant types of work in particular occupations. The respective 'dominant work functions' and the composition of the samples are presented in Table 6.

In an industrial enterprise, 20-26 percent of the total number of workers are engaged in the basic process of industry, i.e. in direct material production. A very similar percentage of workers in both countries (Hungary 29 and Poland 23 percent) is occupied with the

TABLE 6
The Composition of the Samples with Regard to the Dominant Occupational Categories

Specification	Hungary	Poland
	%	%
1. Direct material production	30	26
2. Simple servicing of material production	16	16
3. Complex servicing of material production	13	7
4. Direct organizing and managing of material production	6	5
5. Servicing the process of management	9	9
6. Technological contribution to the production process	4	4
7. Contribution to the scientific basis of the production process	1	1
8. Lack of dominant task	21	32

simple or complex servicing of production. The number of workers who deal with organizing production, with servicing of production and with the technological and scientific preparation of production amounts to about one-fifth of the total. The remaining 21 percent of Hungarian workers and 32 percent of Polish workers have no dominant task in their work. Of these, half of them in both countries (Hungary 11 and Poland 16 percent) have two functions, and the remainder have three functions or more. Data indicate that the carrying out of two functions occurs predominantly among workers engaged in direct material production (Hungary 5 and Poland 11 percent). Such workers are occupied with the simple servicing of material production, while slightly less time is spent on the complex servicing of material production. The relation of the dominant task and the required amount of effort is presented in Table 7.

TABLE 7
Relation between the Dominant Task and Estimates of the Amount of Effort Required

Specification	Hungary	Poland
	(Cramer V)	
1. Level of required physical effort	0.38	0.30
2. Degree of monotony of physical effort	0.26	0.23
3. Independent decision-making/complexity of instructions obtained	0.29	0.26
4. Complexity of information involved	0.32	0.27
5. Hardship of physical working conditions	0.32	0.27
6. Degree of stress involved		

As indicated by Cramer V values, there is a strong or a fairly strong relation between the type of dominant task and the kind and level of effort demanded from a worker in a given occupation. This relation is stronger in Hungary than in Poland, which points to a greater consistency in Hungarian estimates and descriptions of occupations.

According to the estimates obtained, there exists an even stronger relation, measured by Cramer V, between the dominant task of a given occupation and the required level of knowledge and professional competence, as well as between the dominant function and level of education:

	Hungary	Poland
Level of required knowledge	0.35	0.31
Level of professional competence	0.34	0.27
Level of education	0.30	0.29

The required levels of professional competence are very similar in both countries. The process of selection of workers for given occupations, carried out according to the level of education and the work required, results in a state of consistency between the respective requirements and levels of education in both countries.

In the classification presented, the particular occupations selected with respect to their work content are also distinct in terms of the type of work involved. The tasks entailed by these occupations determine the concrete requirements to be met — i.e., level of education and professional competence. As indicated in Table 7, there is a distinct relation between the dominant function and the hardship of working conditions, especially physical hardship. The relation is a little weaker with regard to nervous strain.

The characteristic social composition of the workers actually occupying the jobs in question points to the fact that the division of labour, determined by the content of work, functions as a mechanism of social selection but not only with regard to professional competence.

In both countries there is a relationship between the dominant function and the worker's sex (Cramer V in Hungary = 0.21, and in Poland = 0.25). As expected, the function that is particularly feminized is the servicing of managerial processes (Hungary 77 and Poland 66 percent). In both countries there is a particularly large ratio of women engaged in direct material production — in Hungary in jobs that have no single dominant task, and in Poland among workers engaged in the simple servicing of the material production process.

With respect to age, the data show low correlations, yet some characteristic deviations can be observed in the composition of workers appointed to certain jobs. In Poland the highest ratio of the oldest age group is found among those who have no simple dominant task at work and those occupied with the simple servicing of material production; in Hungary the highest ratio can be found in simple servicing and in the organization and management of production.

Occupations that are viewed unfavourably in society with regard to content of work (simple servicing of the production process; servicing of management; and those lacking a dominant task) are more often taken up by a 'socially weaker' category of workers than would seem to be the case if the distribution reflected the composition of the samples. At the same time, both sets of data indicate that, in jobs concerned with the simple servicing of material production and lacking a dominant function, we also find the highest ratio of people with the lowest pay. In the case of industrial workers dealing with the simple servicing of material production, low pay can perhaps be explained by the simple nature of the work. However, such an explanation is inadequate for occupations that lack a dominant task. The cause of this situation may be inherent in the very 'social weakness' of the workers employed in such positions.

The proclivity of the workers for a given category of occupations, selected with respect to the content of work, is strongly related to whether it is carried out in a one-, two- or multi-shift system. In both countries it is primarily manual workers, occupied with direct material production and its simple servicing, as well as organizers and managers of the production process (Hungary 18 and Poland 29 percent), who are employed in the most arduous three-shift system. The workers in the remaining occupations, among whom non-manual workers predominate (about 90 percent), are employed in the more favourable one-shift system of work.

In both countries there is little relation between the worker's dominant function and his or her attitude to work. There exists hardly any relation between this function and the intensity of rejection of great physical effort. However, respondents' answers were significantly irregular. The most negative attitude was characteristic of a high proportion (above 60 percent in both countries) of those engaged in direct material production, but in Poland it was also high among organizers and managers of the production process.

There is also no relation between the dominant occupational function and the intensity of rejection of great mental effort. According to respondents' answers in both countries, the highest amount of rejection is found among workers engaged in direct production. Neither is there any relation between the dominant function and work satisfaction, the importance attached to promotion, improvement of qualifications or pay increases. Therefore the division of labour does not determine either the level of work satisfaction or estimated prospects.

The content of work, defined by its dominant task, exerts an important influence on such factors as the amount of effort applied, the necessary preparation of workers, and working conditions (physical hardship and nervous strain, organization of working time). The content of work thus functions as a specific mechanism for the allocation of workers to particular jobs, but this operates more systematically in relation to their preparation for work and more selectively in respect of demographic features. Although the relation between the content of work and the level of pay is small, the socially weaker category of workers (defined by demographic features such as sex and age) is shifted to unattractive working positions. The fact that other sources of differentiation overlap with the content of work disturbs any clear connection between attitudes to work and the content of work. This is similar to the finding of A. Sarapata's study on workers' attitudes towards job automation.[6] Sarapata did not find any substantial differences. Such attitudes are modified by other factors not analysed here.

POSITION IN MANAGEMENT

The position occupied in the system of management of an industrial enterprise is the third element in the differentiation of the workers' situation and results directly from the social division of labour. The following three categories were employed: (1) subordinate workers; (2) executives of the lowest rank (having no subordinates among their personnel who also had others working under them); and (3) superiors of higher ranks. The last category comprises directors of industrial enterprises who represent a very small group in the samples in both countries.

In both countries the proportions of the three different categories of posts that have been used are nearly identical. Subordinate workers occupy 77 percent of all posts, executives of a lower rank 18 and 19 percent, and superiors of higher rank 5 and 4 percent. The composition of these groups with regard to sex was also similar. In Hungary, 52 percent of subordinate workers were women and in Poland 49 percent, 28 percent of executives were women (Poland 21 percent). In both countries, the higher the post in the hierarchy, the smaller the number of women. Where age is concerned the highest proportion of subordinate workers are young workers whereas middle-aged workers (30-44 years) constitute the highest proportion of superiors of a higher rank. In Hungary the highest proportion of lower-rank executives were middle-aged, but in Poland such posts were occupied by an older age group.

In both countries age and sex affect the selection of workers to executive and managerial posts and there was no relation between the position occupied in the structure of management and social background. However, there was a correlation between the period of time devoted to professional preparation and level of education attained, although workers' length of service within an enterprise had a smaller effect on promotion to a higher post. In each country and each social category, professional experience was of different importance. In Hungary the relation between occupational experience and appointment to a white-collar or professional post is 0.21 and 0.23, but in Poland this positive relationship exists for all social categories, including unskilled and skilled workers. In both countries, although more so in Poland, the holding of a superior post is related to affiliation to the Workers' Party.

The selection of workers for higher posts in management is determined to a greater extent by acquired rather than inherited features, with the exception of sex. The appointment to a superior post is more closely related to level of education than to experience within the enterprise. In Poland professional experience is important for selection to higher posts in all socio-occupational categories, but in Hungary professional experience counts only in the non-manual categories.

Separate analysis of each of the four social categories indicates a relation between the worker's position in the managerial system and the level of independent decision-making required and complexity of instructions involved. However, this relation varies according to social category, as the respective Cramer V values

TABLE 8
The Effect of the Worker's Position in the Managerial System on the Two Variables of Authority

	Independent decision-making		Complexity of instructions	
	Hungary	Poland	Hungary	Poland
Unskilled workers	0.19	0.18	0.18	0.18
Skilled workers	0.22	0.18	0.15	0.18
White-collar workers	0.30	0.29	0.29	0.21
Professionals	0.26	0.24	0.27	0.16

show in Table 8. The values indicate that, if a worker belongs to a particular social category, this has a significant differentiating effect on content of work with regard to position in the structure of management. In both categories of manual workers, the exercise of executive functions (mainly of a lower rank) does not coincide with mental work. It is probable that the decisions are of a simple character and fall within a narrow range. The complexity of instructions dealt with by executive-skilled workers may be lower than those of subordinate skilled workers engaged in the technically complex aspects of production. Essentially, the difference between the non-executive type of work and executive skilled work is small.

This issue is more important for professionals, as a greater proportion of them occupy posts of higher rank in the managerial structure and therefore have to take wide-ranging decisions with complex consequences. Nevertheless, Polish experts doubt whether the instructions with which the higher-level professionals deal really require a greater mental effort, as Cramer V is the lowest for this category (0.16). On the other hand, in the white-collar category, where tasks are simple, a greater mental effort is required with regard to independent decision-making and the complexity of instructions, when taking over a higher post.

It is important to note that such differences exist even if the attempted interpretation is not completely valid. Entry into the management of an enterprise does not have identical consequences for members of manual and non-manual categories with regard to content of work.

INEQUALITIES BETWEEN MEN AND WOMEN

As sex functions as a factor in selection for executive and managerial posts, it is worth considering this problem with regard to level of pay. The relation between pay and sex at three selected points on the hierarchy generates the following Cramer V values:

	Hungary	Poland
Subordinate workers	0.35	0.41
Low-rank executives	0.37	0.44
Superiors of higher rank	0.24	0.46

The association is very strong, and the level of pay obtained by women is lower. However, some divergences exist between Hungary and Poland, as in Hungary the relationship is systematically weaker than in Poland. In Hungary discrimination against women in respect of earnings is lowest in the higher ranks of management but in Poland it is at its highest there. In Poland discrimination increases from the lowest to the highest category within management, but in Hungary discrimination is at its highest among lower-rank executives.

Investigations were carried out in 1979, and in the second half of

1980 the level of pay in Poland was raised considerably. Many industrial enterprises applied the progressive principle in allocating pay increases, and therefore the relation may have become weaker. However, this may then have had more effect on subordinate than executive posts.

The present analysis indicates no relation between respondents' sex and their subjective prospects concerning pay increases. In Poland, Cramer's V amounts to values below 0.11 in all three categories, but in Hungary the values are 0.09 for subordinate workers, 0.13 for lower-rank executives and 0.24 for superiors of higher ranks. In both countries discrimination against women in respect of earnings coincided with men's expectations about their own prospects for pay increases. Such shared male values have a rather pejorative implication. It seems that, particularly in Poland, expectations in general resulted from people's lack of hope of obtaining a more just payment distribution policy and indicate a common view that the policy has petrified.

Is the respondent's sex a factor that leads to differential importance being attached to significant features of executive and managerial types of work, i.e., responsibility, organizational activity and independence?

Importance attached to responsibility at work does not depend on sex in any of the categories. In Hungary the highest Cramer V value (obtained by low-rank executives) amounts only to 0.11. There is a similar lack of relation between sex and the importance attached to organizational activity (with the exception in Hungary of lower-rank executives where V = 0.22). The situation is identical with respect to the importance attached to independence at work, as a slightly stronger association occurs only in Hungary among lower-rank executives.

The system of values, analysed with regard to the importance assigned to essential features of executive and managerial posts, is similar for men and women. There is no difference between the sexes in their willingness to carry out tasks that require independence and responsibility. In the professional structure of management these differences occur between categories of workers irrespective of sex.

JOB SATISFACTION

The analysis carried out within each social category indicates little relation between the worker's actual position and job satisfaction in the manual worker's category. In Poland there is a weak relationship for white-collar workers (V = 0.09 and less), and in Hungary it is only a very little stronger (V = 0.16). However, the satisfaction that the professionals derive from work does depend more heavily on the position occupied in the system of management (V = 0.24 and 0.21).

TABLE 9
Work Satisfaction, According to Social Category

Specification	Wholly satisfied	Fairly satisfied	Partly satisfied — partly dissatisfied	Wholly or rather dissatisfied	Total
	%	%	%	%	%
Hungary					
1. Unskilled workers	23	43	32	2	100
2. Skilled workers	21	46	31	2	100
3. White-collar workers	15	50	33	2	100
4. Professionals	8	55	32	5	100
Poland					
1. Unskilled workers	43	33	21	3	100
2. Skilled workers	35	37	24	4	100
3. White-collar workers	34	39	25	2	100
4. Professionals	15	47	30	8	100

In both countries and in all social categories a majority of workers declared that they experienced job satisfaction. Dissatisfaction occured only sporadically and was less than 8 percent in all samples. It is worthwhile mentioning that the present proportion of those dissatisfied with work has decreased when compared with 1974. Then, according to A. Sarapata's study, 11 percent were dissatisfied, while according to our survey there were only 3-4 percent expressing dissatisfaction.[7]

A year after these investigations had been carried out, the workers' protests broke out in Poland. Apart from the changes sought for the whole society, workers put forward numerous claims regarding basic working conditions, such as working hours, safety at work, organization of work, etc. As conditions could not have worsened to a very great extent during a single year, it is obvious that workers were not at all satisfied with their work — they were only tolerating existing working conditions and bad social organization. Once again, it was shown that answers to questions on workers' satisfaction are of little predictive value.[8]

FUTURE PROSPECTS

As workers' prospects for improvement in the social situation and in working conditions are an essential element in their evaluation of work, such expectations and the chances of their realization were investigated. Workers' aspirations for promotion, for pay increases and for improvement of qualifications were analysed in terms of their importance to the workers and with regard to the probability of their realization. Two factors should be noted here: the promotion ladder is not equally long for different socio-occupational categories — it is shortest for unskilled workers. Second, in theory, the intelligentsia is the category that has the smallest opportunities for advancement (owing to the high level already achieved). However, the increase of wages seems to be the most variable factor,[9] and can obviously affect all (see Table 10). In Hungary only unskilled and white-collar workers are close to each other in respect of expectations about pay increases. In Poland expectations of promotion are similar among skilled workers and white-collar workers, whereas expectations about pay increases are similar among skilled workers and professionals.

In Poland and Hungary the estimates given concerning chances of fulfilment are different. Estimates of chances of promotion are similar, if not identical, among skilled and white-collar workers in Hungary, and skilled workers and professionals viewed their chances of pay increases in the same way. However, unskilled workers were particularly optimistic where pay increases were concerned. In Poland identical estimates concerning pay increases occur among professionals and white-collar workers. All the other aspects of future prospects varied according to social category.

With regard to all three kinds of chances, the optimism of professionals was matched only by the white-collar workers. Hungarian workers are culturally differentiated, yet in Hungarian industry they are given similar chances to realize future prospects. Polish workers are culturally unified to a greater extent, yet they perceive their future prospects in a more differentiated manner.

TABLE 10
Future Prospects: Social Categories According to Importance Attached to, and Estimated Opportunities for Improving Various Aspects of the Work Situation*

Aspect of Work Situation	Hungary	Poland
Promotion		
Importance	4,3,2,1	4,2—3,1
Estimated opportunities	4,2 = 3,1	4,3,2,1
Pay Increase		
Importance	2,4,1 = 3	2 = 4,1,3
Estimated opportunities	1 = 2 = 4,4	4 = 3,2,1
Improvement of Skills		
Importance	4,2—3,1	4,3,2,1
Estimated opportunities	4,2,3,1	3,4,2,1
Total Prospects		
Importance	4,2 = 3,1	4,2 = 3,1
Estimated opportunities	4,2,3,1	4—3,2,1

*Social categories: 1. unskilled and semi-skilled workers
2. skilled workers
3. white collar workers
4. professionals

Categories according to decreasing value of mean evaluation (on a 9-point scale) : symbol (=) means a difference within the limit of 0.05 points; symbol (—) means a difference within the limit of 0.10 points.

The data in Table 11 show that the greatest importance is attached to pay increases in all social categories in both countries. This element is considered a significant expression of esteem, and is a factor that strengthens the worker's position and improves the situation of the family. In Hungary the total degree of importance attached to all three elements reaches into the top half of the scale, but in Poland they moved into the top third of the scale, which seems to indicate a more intense orientation towards the future. In the light of the data, the difference existing in Poland between aspirations and opportunities becomes an important problem, for with regard to promotion and pay increases, the differences between the average values are smaller in Hungary. With regard to the improvement of qualifications, the actual chances in Hungarian industry exceed the level of workers' needs, but in Polish industry the importance attached to the improvement of qualifications exceeds the level of opportunities for its realization. We can conclude, therefore, that a feeling of hopelessness on the part of Polish workers leads to intense frustration, but no work dissatisfaction as such was indicated in our investigations.

TABLE 11

Future Prospects: Importance Attached to, and Expectations of, Obtaining Promotion, Pay Increase and Improvement of Qualifications According to Social Category (arithmetical means calculated from a 9-point scale)

	Hungary				Poland			
Specification	Unskilled workers	Skilled workers	White-collar workers	Profes-sionals	Unskilled workers	Skilled workers	White-collar workers	Profes-sionals
Promotion								
Importance attached to	3.15	3.32	3.84	4.64	5.43	6.55	6.45	6.73
Estimated chances of	2.32	2.59	2.56	3.44	2.70	3.44	3.63	4.02
Differences between arithmetical means	0.83	0.73	1.28	1.20	2.73	3.11	2.82	2.71
Pay increases								
Importance attached to	5.93	6.44	5.89	6.32	7.30	7.55	7.26	7.54
Estimated chances of	3.80	3.77	3.48	3.72	3.59	3.79	4.01	4.03
Differences between arithmetical means	2.13	2.67	2.41	2.60	3.71	3.76	3.25	3.51
Improvement of qualifications								
Importance attached to	3.81	4.80	4.74	5.33	5.06	6.47	6.69	7.30
Estimated chances of	4.15	4.96	4.71	5.36	3.80	5.03	5.53	5.37
Differences between arithmetical means	−0.34	−0.16	0.03	−0.03	1.26	1.44	1.16	1.93
Future prospects: total								
Importance attached to	4.27	4.85	4.82	5.43	5.93	6.85	6.80	7.19
Estimated chances of	3.42	3.77	3.58	4.17	3.36	4.08	4.39	4.47
Differences between arithmetical means	0.85	1.08	1.24	1.26	2.57	2.77	2.41	2.62

CONCLUSIONS

Several conclusions of a general character can be drawn from our investigations.

It was confirmed that physical effort is still a specific feature of the occupations of manual workers and indeed is their defining characteristic (although manual effort is a requirement of all the categories, it varies significantly in intensity). Mental effort, however, is not a specific feature of non-manual work alone. It is a requirement in all socio-occupational categories, although again it varies in intensity,[10] and important forms of social differentiation are generated by the social division of labour.

In general, all social categories consider heavy physical effort a burdensome factor and instead evaluate mental effort positively, if it leads to self-actualization, or the strengthening of one's position (independence, decision-making, etc.). The greater the intellectual elements in work, the higher the estimate of the mental effort involved. Differences in the level of positive evaluations of such effort are greater between the social categories in each country than between countries.

The content of work consistently determines the type and intensity of effort required from workers and the level of professional qualification demanded. Therefore, the content of work functions as a mechanism for the selection and distribution of workers to particular occupations according to qualifications. The content of work also determines the allocation of 'socially weaker' workers to unattractive positions and may determine other working conditions (such as physical hardship and organization of working time). However, no relationship was indicated between the content of work and workers' attitudes with respect to other features (such as job satisfaction, prospects for pay increases, etc.).

The analysis of the different social categories of workers with regard to their positions in the managerial system of an enterprise points to the great importance played by the factor of sex. The higher the workers' category in the structure of management, the lower the proportion of women. However, the worker's social background was not found to be a mechanism of selection in this respect. Our investigations confirm the existence of strong discrimination against women as regards level of pay, but this is not reflected in women having lower estimates about their future chances of pay increases. Appointment of a worker to a higher post does not necessarily coincide with the need for a greater amount of intellectual effort. Promotion opportunities vary according to social category, with chances being particularly reduced for executive manual workers.

Future prospects are differentiated according to social category. At the same time there is a strong, though more equally distributed, orientation towards promotion. This may generate feelings of being blocked in the improvement of individual life chances. This appears, however, to exert a rather weak effect on expressions of dissatisfaction with work.

NOTES

1. J. Kulpińska, 'Koncepcje sytuacji pracy w badaniach struktury społecznej', *Przeglad Socjologiczny* ('The Concept of Work Situation in Investigations on Social Structure'), *Sociological Review*, vol. XXXII, no. 2.
2. J. Forslin, A. Sarapata and A.M. Whitehall (eds), *Automation and Industrial Workers, A Fifteen Nation Study*, vol. 1, part 1, Pergamon Press, London, 1979. In order to investigate the problems discussed in this chapter, some measures designed for the research project, 'Automation and Industrial Workers', were used. They were proposed by Dr M. Loetsch and Dr W.W. Kołbanowski, who participated in both cross-national studies. See W.I. Usenin and W.W. Krewiewicz (eds), *Working Class under the Conditions of Scientific and Technical Revolution* (in Russian), Moscow, 1979.
3. M.L. Kohn, *Class and Conformity. A Study in Values*, 2nd ed., University of Chicago Press, 1977.
4. See W. Jadow and W. Zdradomystow (eds), *Man and His Work* (in Russian), Moscow, 1967.
5. S. Kowalewska, 'Charakter pracy a uczestnictwo w kulturze', (Character of Work and the Participation in Culture'), in G.W. Osipowa (ed.), *Społeczne problemy pracy i produkcji pod red* (Social Problems of Work and Production), J. Szczepańskiego, Warszawa, 1970.
6. Forslin, Sarapata and Whitehall, op. cit., p. 151.
7. Ibid., p. 132.
8. See A. Sarapata (ed.), *Problematyka i metody badań nad zadowoleniem z pracy* (Problems of Work Satisfaction and Applied Research Techniques), Wrocław, 1973; and D. Dobrowolska, *Praca w życiu człowieka* (Work in Man's Life), Warsaw, 1980.

9. K. Bursche, *Awans robotników w zakładzie przemysłowym* (The Advancement of Workers in Industrial Enterprises), Warsaw, 1973; A. Preiss, *Technicy — robotnicy w załogach przemysłowych* (Technicians — Workers among Industrial Employees). Warsaw, 1976.

10. T. Kotarbiński, *Sprawność i błąd* (Efficiency and Error), Warsaw, 1966.

3

DIFFERENCES IN WELFARE

Lidia Beskid and Tamás Kolosi

Our intention in comparing material conditions of life in Hungary and Poland is to draw attention to the more important tendencies in social differentiation that characterize the two countries. Differentiation of socio-occupational categories was found but also other differences distinguished between the two nations. Owing to the limitations of the basic research design the information obtained is illustrative rather than complete.

The objective data provided by the respondents were, from the methodological point of view, restricted. However, we assume that other investigations carried out under identical circumstances and using the same methods would produce a similar range of error.

Income differentials represent a kind of intermediary between work and material living conditions, as they are connected with the position occupied in the occupational distribution and are a component of the income accrued per person (household member — i.e., the role which most directly reflects material living conditions). Factor analysis has shown that the relationship between earnings and occupational category is stronger than the relationship between earnings and living conditions.

Such analysis indicates that earnings should be viewed more as a financial expression of differentiation within occupational structure than as a direct determinant of living conditions.

Actual material living conditions are connected not with an individual but rather with a family and with household composition. Only certain major components of material living conditions were analysed: household income, household conditions, and possession of specified consumer durable goods. We also attempted to discover correlations and interrelationships between these factors.

Actual living conditions in a given society are also considerably affected by other factors, such as the system of retail prices, assortment of goods available, welfare payments and their principles of allocation, extra earnings, time-budget and consumption habits. Such factors have a significant effect, particularly in a socialist country, on the living conditions of society as a whole and of each social category within it. As we did not take such factors into account, the results of our investigation simply reveal basic tendencies in the quantitative aspects of living conditions.

EARNINGS STRUCTURE

Respondents' earnings are made up of a mean monthly salary, bonus rewards and overtime pay. Since the level of earnings was determined on the basis of responses to questionnaires, the possible range of error due to subjective factors was large. Previous surveys have shown that intentional mis-statement is not evenly distributed, but increases with the level of earnings. Unintended mis-statements, on the other hand, may arise from the difficulty of totting-up all annual earnings.

Two aspects of respondents' earnings were analysed:

1. the factors associated with income differentials between industrial workers and those operative within particular categories;
2. The distribution of earnings, where regression functions and correlation coefficients were the basis for studying differentiation within the social categories. The following characteristics were taken into consideration: sex, age, education, housing conditions, occupation, strenuousness of work, shift work and socio-political activity.

The following conclusions were drawn.

1. Sex exerts a profound effect on the level of earnings in both countries. Although the direction of influence was similar in all social categories, the importance of the effect was not the same. In Poland differentiation on sex lines was largest among skilled workers and in Hungary was largest among unskilled and semi-

skilled workers. In Table 1 the coefficients r and r^2 (in brackets) show the correlation between sex and the level of earnings.

TABLE 1
Correlation between Sex and Level of Earnings

	Hungary	Poland
All workers	0.47(0.23)*	0.46(0.21)
Unskilled and semi-skilled workers	0.42(0.17)	0.46(0.22)
Skilled workers	0.42(0.17)	0.51(0.25)
White-collar workers	0.48(0.24)	0.45(0.20)
Professionals	0.42(0.18)	0.39(0.15)

*r^2 in brackets.

2. The most important factor in accounting for income differentials among white-collar workers, and in particular among professionals, is the worker's occupational position (Hungary r = 0.52 and 0.62, and Poland r = 0.54 and 0.59) — a similar phenomenon in both countries. Earnings in these categories also depended on age. Particularly among professionals, the exercising of a managerial function is a vital factor in the receipt of higher salaries. For white-collar workers with secondary education, this influence upon the level of earnings is greater than that of sex. The impact of occupational position on income differentials in Poland and Hungary varies between the two countries. In Poland occupational positions are more important among skilled workers, whereas in Hungary this is the case among unskilled and semi-skilled workers.

3. The effect of age can be observed mainly among skilled workers and is similar in both countries. In Poland age does not affect unskilled and semi-skilled workers' earnings in any significant way and in Hungary there is a negative correlation.

4. Another factor that explains differences in earnings is the correlation between socio-political activity and the level of earnings. The analysis shows a strong positive correlation among white-collar

workers in Hungary (r = 0.36) and among professionals in Poland (r = 0.39).

5. For methodological reasons the impact of education on income differentials can be analysed only on the basis of results for the whole samples. An association between education and earnings is a basic feature in both countries. In Hungary this dependence is stronger than in Poland (Hungary r = 0.33, Poland r = 0.17), and it is also reflected within each social category as a factor associated with internal income differentials (Hungary r = 0.37, Poland r = 0.17).

6. This result is related to the correlation established between the intellectual complexity of work and the level of earnings (Table 2). In Poland the correlation of these variables is almost identical for all investigated categories. In Hungary the correlation between the intellectual complexity of work and earnings is insignificant among manual workers, but increases substantially among white-collar workers and professionals.

TABLE 2
Correlation between the Intellectual Complexity of Work and the Level of Earnings

	Hungary	Poland
All workers	0.39	0.30
Unskilled and semi-skilled workers	0.11	0.24
Skilled workers	0.18	0.28
White-collar workers	0.38	0.29
Professionals	0.33	0.28

7. In both Hungary and Poland housing conditions are negatively correlated with earnings. In Hungary this relationship is not significant, but in Poland the size of homes is affected by the earnings of both manual and non-manual workers.

In conclusion, we can say the basic features of a worker's status, such as sex, age, education, housing conditions, occupational position, intellectual complexity of work, and socio-political activity, are significantly related to income differentials within each category.[1] However, these relationships become increasingly pronounced as the educational level of subjects rises. R^2 for a composite of the above variables is shown in Table 3.[2] On average, the factors that are related to income differentials within the various social categories have greater force in Hungary than in Poland. In Poland, except for sex, sociologists have failed to find factors that significantly differentiate between the earnings of the unskilled and semi-skilled category. It seems that, among other things, explanations should be looked for in terms of how income differentials are themselves established.[3]

TABLE 3
Multiple Correlation between Level of Earnings and Six Variables of Social Status

	Hungary	Poland
All workers	0.47	0.37
Unskilled and semi-skilled workers	0.33	0.29
Skilled workers	0.38	0.40
White-collar workers	0.53	0.56
Professionals	0.61	0.57

However, we consider the differences in earnings between professionals and white-collar workers in Hungary and Poland to have been explained satisfactorily. The factors primarily responsible are occupational position, age (more important in Hungary), sex and socio-political activity, which are strongly correlated with the earnings of professionals and white-collar workers in both countries.

What distinguishes the system of earnings in Poland from that in Hungary are the weaker correlations between earnings and the socio-occupational categories, education and work, and complexity and shift work. These produce a better account of the differences in earnings between the social categories in Hungary. Average pay in industry is low (see Table 4). The difference between the average earnings of unskilled and semi-skilled workers is greater in Hungary than in Poland (owing to a large number of women in the structure of the sample). In Poland white-collar workers' and professionals' incomes exceed average pay rates to a higher extent than in Hungary.

TABLE 4
Differentiation of the Average Earnings of Four Social Categories

	Hungary	Poland
Unskilled and semi-skilled workers	88.3	95.3
Skilled workers	104.3	104.8
White-collar workers	102.2	107.2
Professionals	134.7	137.2

The distribution of earnings in Poland and Hungary was analysed with special regard to any irregularity of distribution within and between the various social categories. This was found to be rather different in the two countries, as Table 5 reveals.

1. The range of earnings between the extremes of the distribution is larger in Poland than in Hungary. Among the respondents the average pay of the top 10 percent with the highest earnings is 3.12 times higher in Poland than the bottom 10 percent with the lowest earnings (Hungary, 2.81 times higher). Similar differences in the distribution of earnings are evident in all the socio-occupational categories.

2. Irregularities within the total distribution are somewhat lower in Poland than in Hungary ($M_2 : M_1$). However, in Poland this is considerably higher in the skilled workers' category and a little higher in the professional category. The distribution of earnings according to level was analysed in further detail by means of a 9

point scale. The first point on the distribution line corresponds to the average pay of the bottom 10 percent (those with the lowest earnings) and the ninth point corresponds to the average pay of the top 10 percent (those with the highest earnings). The points on this scale enable a comparison of the distribution of earnings without reference to their real financial value. The comparison of the absolute values of earnings in two different currencies is therefore avoided.

TABLE 5
Indices of Irregularity in the Distribution of Earnings

Social categories	Hungary $\frac{M_2}{M_1}$	Hungary $\frac{M_1}{M}$	Hungary $\frac{M_2}{M}$	Hungary $\frac{D_{10}}{D_1}$	Poland $\frac{M_2}{M_1}$	Poland $\frac{M_1}{M}$	Poland $\frac{M_2}{M}$	Poland $\frac{D_{10}}{D_1}$
All workers	1.70	0.77	1.31	2.81	1.67	0.78	1.30	3.12
Unskilled workers	1.65	0.80	1.32	2.72	1.64	0.77	1.26	3.03
Skilled workers	1.49	0.80	1.19	2.51	1.66	0.76	1.26	3.04
White-collar workers	1.74	0.77	1.34	3.08	1.71	0.75	1.28	3.21
Professionals	1.60	0.78	1.25	2.99	1.67	0.76	1.27	3.13

M: arithmetical mean of all respondents' earnings
M_1: arithmetical mean of earnings in the bracket $m_i < M$ where m_i is earnings: and i is the respondent
M_2: arithmetical mean of earnings in the bracket $m_1 \geqslant \hat{M}$
D_1: arithmetical mean of earnings of the 10% lowest earnings
D_{10}: arithmetical mean of earnings of the 10% highest earnings

Figure 1 shows the distribution of earnings for individual categories of workers in Hungary and Poland according to the nine distribution points.

1. In both countries the distribution curve for the three successive categories is similar to the logarithmic-normal curve. In Poland the mutual conditioning of the curves is stronger than in Hungary. The curve representing the earnings of professionals is different in both countries (in Hungary it is close to the exponential pattern).

FIGURE 1
Curves of Earnings Distribution

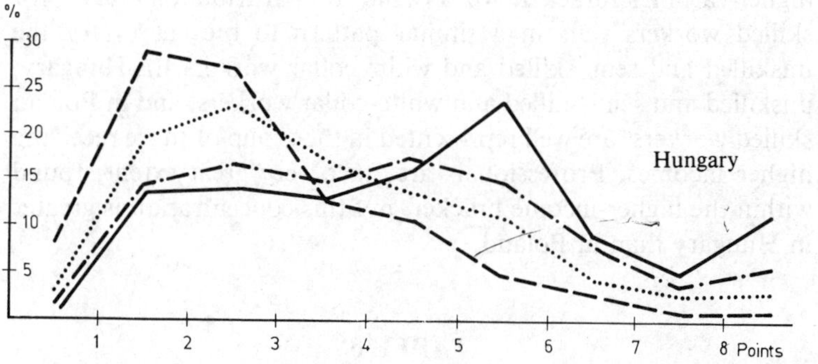

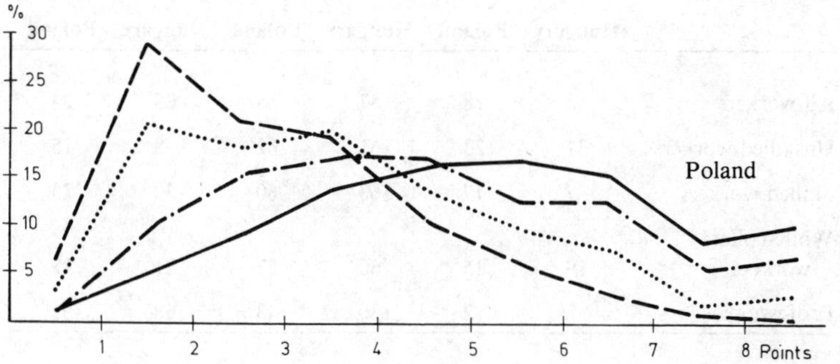

Key

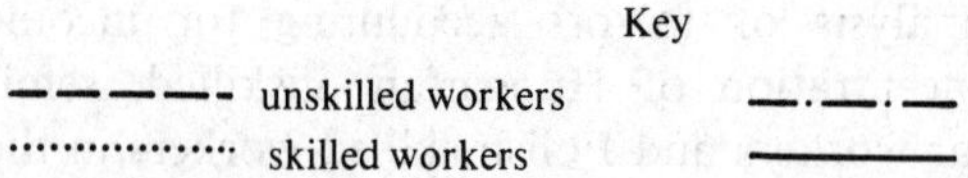

2. The relations between the distribution curves for the different social categories vary for the two countries (see Table 6). In Hungary the distribution curve for skilled workers runs between those of the unskilled and semi-skilled workers and the professionals. The curve for the white-collar (secondary education) workers runs above that of the skilled workers in the lower-income bracket and below that of the skilled workers in the average and higher-earnings bracket. In Poland the distribution curve for skilled workers runs in a similar pattern to the curves for the unskilled and semi-skilled and white-collar workers. In Hungary, unskilled and semi-skilled and white-collar workers, and in Poland skilled workers, are well represented in the group of those receiving higher incomes. Professionals are, to a very great extent, found within the higher-income bracket, but this concentration is greater in Hungary than in Poland.

TABLE 6
Distribution of Earnings, According to Social Category

Social categories	Low earnings		Middle earnings		High earnings	
	Hungary	Poland	Hungary	Poland	Hungary	Poland
All workers	18	18	57	58	25	24
Unskilled workers	31	23	61	62	8	15
Skilled workers	7	17	63	60	30	23
White-collar workers	19	15	60	57	21	28
Professionals	2	2	30	43	68	55

Note. With the use of the 9-point scale it has been assumed that:
low earnings = points 1, 2
middle earnings = points 3, 4, 5
high earnings = points 6, 7, 8, 9.

Conclusions are more precise if a worker's occupational position is included in the analysis of factors accounting for income differentials. The concentration of Hungarian unskilled, semi-skilled and white-collar workers and Polish skilled workers in the low-earnings bracket applies only to workers who have no subordinates. Similarly, the concentration of professionals in the high-earnings bracket predominantly applies to people who do have subordinates. The concentration of professionals in this category is twice as high in Hungary as in Poland (see Table 7).

TABLE 7
Coefficients of Deviation from the Proportional Share of Earnings

Social categories	Low earnings		Middle earnings		High earnings	
	Hungary	Poland	Hungary	Poland	Hungary	Poland
Unskilled workers						
with no subordinates	2.03	1.29	0.88	1.00	0.19	0.67
with subordinates	0.61	0.29	1.10	1.05	1.35	1.59
Skilled workers						
with no subordinates	0.61	1.06	1.16	1.04	0.88	0.80
with subordinates	0.09	0.22	1.28	0.85	1.48	2.38
White-collar workers						
with no subordinates	1.61	1.28	0.86	1.09	0.15	0.42
with subordinates	0.10	0.59	1.23	1.00	1.87	1.47
Professionals						
with no subordinates	0.47	0.24	1.03	0.96	2.36	1.92
with subordinates of higher level	—	0.02	0.47	0.41	8.24	3.76

Note: Coefficients have been calculated as a quotient of the share of a given category in a specified bracket of earnings, by the share of that category in the general structure. The bracket of low earnings includes points 1, 2; points 3, 4, 5 = middle earnings; points 6, 7, 8, 9 = high earnings.

HOUSEHOLD INCOME

The average income of all household members was also analysed. This income arises from: earnings of all occupationally active household members, overtime pay, extra earnings and welfare allowances such as family benefits, pensions and scholarships. The average income per household member was calculated on the basis of the total household income. However, to use the average income in this way does gloss over the impact of various demographic factors on household wealth. It does not, for example, take into account individual needs of family members determined by age. Similarly, it cannot take into account how general expenses are shared out, or allow for the fact that a high gross household income makes it possible to save relatively large sums of money even given a low income per family member. Despite these shortcomings, the average income value is used internationally and is easy to calculate. Here both the factors producing income differentials and the effects they in turn produced were also considered.

Firstly, the magnitude of the different components of household income (gross income, respondent's earnings, other revenue) was analysed separately for men's and women's households. The analysis in both countries shows that 19-25 percent of the variance in income per person can be explained by the mechanism of income accumulation. In Hungary this factor is identical in men's and women's households, but in Poland it is higher in men's households. Male and female earnings have a different effect on the family income, as in both countries men's earnings show a stronger correlation with income per person. In Hungary the differences due to sex are less important because here the husband's type of job is less important than in Poland. The correlation between the level of earnings and the level of income per family member is particularly important at the extremes. The following conclusions can be drawn from the analysis of the influences on the top-most and bottom-most income categories (identically contructed for both countries).

1. There is no correlation between the highest levels of earnings and average household income. In each category, workers with high earnings are in fact least represented in the high-income-per-person bracket (i.e. in the fraction falling above point 8). This clearly shows that demographic factors have a stronger effect on income than earnings of the respondent.[4]

2. There is also a weak correlation between the low level of earnings of the respondent and low income per family member.

3. Any correlation between the level of earnings of the respondent and average income per person is largely restricted to those at middle or rather lower levels. The transition coefficients for respondents with earnings and income up to point 4 on the

distribution scale are shown in Table 8. With the exception of professionals, average and lower earnings determine the family's wealth to quite a large extent.

TABLE 8
Transition Coefficients for Respondents with Earnings and Income up to Point 4 on the Distribution Scale

	Hungary	Poland
Unskilled and semi-skilled workers	0.73	0.73
Skilled workers	0.69	0.69
White-collar workers	0.59	0.56
Professionals	0.54	0.38

Further analysis of the income per person differentials included the following factors:

1. demographic factors (household size and composition, number of children in the same household as the respondent);
2. socio-occupational category, occupational position, difficulty of work and education;
3. factors connected with housing conditions (size and character of dwelling and necessity of commuting).

In both countries the analysis of the regression function shows that demographic household features exert the strongest effect on the level of income per person.

The survey shows that the number of children and the size of a household have the greatest effect on the income per person[5] (see Table 9). There is a strong negative correlation in Poland but a weaker correlation in Hungary. In both countries the impact of the two factors differs according to the category of workers considered. There is a relatively weak correlation among white-collar workers (the lowest income level per person in this category is not correlated with either aspect of family situation), and a very strong correlation among professionals (high incomes per person occur only among childless married couples or couples with one child, while two-children families have average or low incomes). This phenomenon is equally strong in both countries.[6]

TABLE 9
Coefficients of Correlation (*r*) between Income per Person and the Number of Children (1) and the Size of Household (2)

Social categories	Hungary (1)	Hungary (2)	Poland (1)	Poland (2)
All workers	−0.42	−0.36	−0.50	−0.46
Unskilled workers	−0.40	−0.34	−0.50	−0.48
Skilled workers	−0.44	−0.38	−0.49	−0.48
White-collar workers	−0.41	−0.32	−0.44	−0.41
Professionals	−0.57	−0.51	−0.57	−0.61

In Poland and Hungary age is positively correlated with income (that is, income per person differentials) but it is only important in the white-collar social category.

Thus, demographic features, to different degrees, explain the income per person differentiation within the various socio-occupational categories, and are of particular importance for the professional group (see Table 10). Other factors, such as social category or housing conditions, are more important in Poland than in Hungary.

The following comparative conclusions can be drawn.

1. In both countries income per household member is most strongly affected by demographic factors, particularly in families of professionals.

2. All the factors investigated have a stronger differentiating effect in Poland than in Hungary and for all social categories there.

3. In both countries there must be an additional, unidentified, group of factors, that, particularly in Hungary, play an important

part in the process of establishing differentials in income per person: 38 percent of the variance in household income differentiation was accounted for in Poland but only 26 percent in Hungary.

TABLE 10
The Range of Variance of Income per Person Explained by Demographic Factors (R^2)

Social categories	Hungary	Poland
All workers	0.22	0.32
Unskilled workers	0.19	0.31
Skilled workers	0.26	0.36
White-collar workers	0.24	0.34
Professionals	0.48	0.49

TABLE 11
Range of Income per Person between Socio-occupational Categories

	Hungary			Poland		
Social categories	M	M_1	M_2	M	M_1	M_2
All workers	1.00	1.00	1.00	1.00	1.00	1.00
Unskilled workers	0.96	0.94	0.99	0.94	0.93	0.94
Skilled workers	0.96	0.98	0.92	1.01	1.01	1.03
White-collar workers	1.03	1.07	1.00	1.14	1.22	1.11
Professionals	1.23	1.30	1.21	1.36	1.44	1.31

Note: M: arithmetical mean of income per person in the households of all respondents
M_1: arithmetical mean of income per person in the bracket $m_i < M$ where m_i is income per person in household and i is the respondent
M_2: arithmetical mean of income in the bracket $m_1 \geqslant M$

Income distribution and its inequalities were analysed (see Table 11) and the following conclusions were drawn.[7]

In both countries the position of professionals and white-collar workers is essentially different from the position of manual workers with regard to income per person. In Poland the contrast between levels of income in different parts of the social configuration is greater, as the average income per household member in professional families is 46 percent higher than in families of unskilled and semi-skilled workers, compared with a figure of 28 percent in Hungary. The relation of skilled workers to unskilled and semi-skilled workers in this respect is 35 percent higher in Poland and 27 percent higher in Hungary.

In Poland these proportions are due to the particularly high-income position of the households of professionals and white-collar workers (note the beginning of their income distribution lines in Figure 2). In Hungary the curve for professionals' income is not very different from the income curves of other categories, but in Poland the same curve deviates considerably from the income curves of the two groups of manual workers. White-collar workers are found to be 'between' skilled workers and professionals.

TABLE 12
Coefficients of Deviation from Proportional Shares in the Income per Person Distribution, According to Quartiles

Social categories	Q_1		Q_2		Q_3		Q_4	
	Hungary	Poland	Hungary	Poland	Hungary	Poland	Hungary	Poland
Unskilled workers	1.26	1.39	0.99	0.99	0.94	0.92	0.80	0.68
Skilled workers	1.10	1.15	1.00	0.99	0.90	0.95	1.00	0.90
White-collar workers	0.77	0.55	1.15	1.02	1.11	1.18	0.95	1.26
Professionals	0.36	0.22	0.83	1.01	1.22	1.08	1.61	1.71

Note: Indices were calculated as quotients of the share of a given category in the quartile structure by the share of that category in the general structure.

The concentration of the various socio-occupational categories in the low- and high-income brackets is different in Poland and Hungary, and therefore the social structure of successive quartiles in the income distribution was examined (see Table 12). The

FIGURE 2
Curves of the Income per Person Distribution

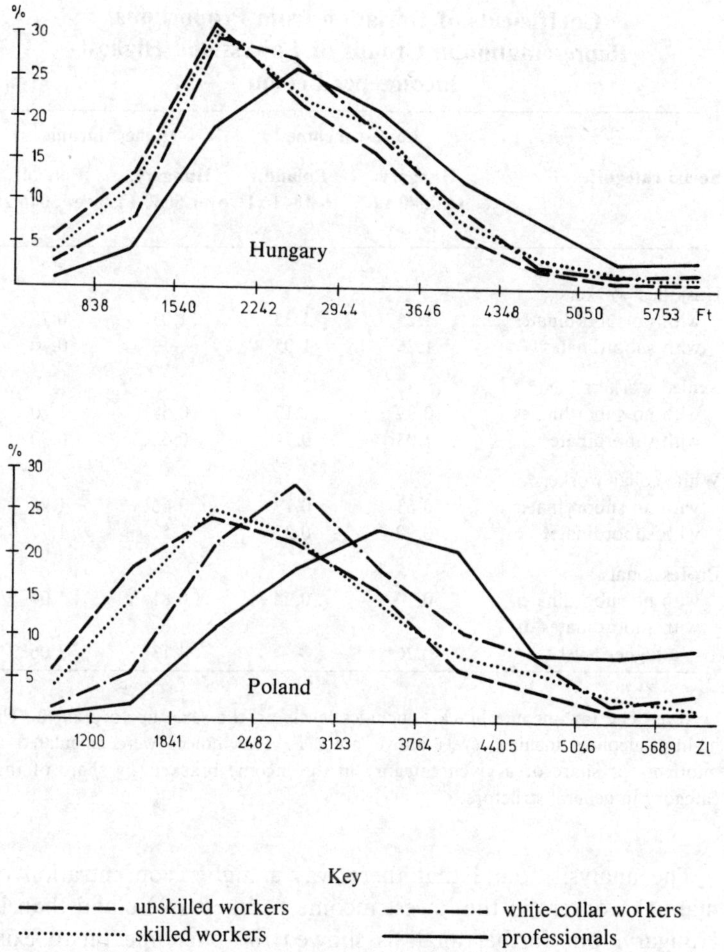

structure of the extreme groups (lowest income per person, up to 1,540 Ft. and 1,841 zł, and highest income per person, up to 5,050 Ft. and 5,046 zł) was also examined to determine what combination of factors produced this deviation from the rest of the social income structure (see Table 13).

TABLE 13
Coefficients of Deviation from Proportional Representation in Groups of Lowest and Highest Income per Person

Social categories	Lowest income		Highest income	
	Hungary: to 1540 Ft.	Poland: to 1841 zł	Hungary: over 5050 Ft.	Poland: over 5046 zł
Unskilled workers				
with no subordinates	1.25	1.33	1.05	0.75
with subordinates	1.26	1.05	—	0.70
Skilled workers				
with no subordinates	0.99	1.13	0.58	1.20
with subordinates	1.03	0.74	0.62	0.80
White-collar workers				
with no subordinates	0.63	0.17	0.66	1.46
with subordinates	0.90	0.32	1.57	1.77
Professionals				
with no subordinates	0.19	0.24	0.81	1.04
with subordinates of a higher level	0.26	—	4.18	3.06

Note: The low-income bracket includes levels on the scale up to point 2. The highest incomes include levels above point 8. The indices were calculated as quotients of share of a given category in the income brackets by share of that category in general structure.

The analysis found that there was a higher concentration of manual workers in the lowest income brackets in Poland than in Hungary, but further analysis showed the phenomenon to exist only among unskilled and semi-skilled workers and among skilled workers with no subordinates. In Poland managerial jobs reduce the possibility of such workers entering the low-income-per-person groups, but in Hungary there is no change in the income-per-person distribution among workers in managerial positions, despite differences in the distribution of earnings.

The analysis also confirmed that there was a high concentration in Poland of professionals and white-collar workers in the highest income brackets. However, the worker's actual function, as an additional variable, introduces differences in the structure of the income distribution in Poland and Hungary. In both countries (though to a greater extent in Hungary than in Poland) there is a stronger concentration of professional managers in the high-income bracket, and a lesser concentration of white-collar managers (although Poland is marked by a higher concentration of white-collar managers than is Hungary).

The following final conclusions can be drawn from the data collected. The differences in income distribution for professionals and white-collar workers (with secondary education) in relation to other workers in Poland and in Hungary are related to the fact that in Poland there is a lower proportion of these two categories in the low-income groups and a higher percentage of workers with no managerial function (particularly those with secondary education) in the high-income brackets.

In both countries inequalities in the income-per-person distribution are higher than the inequalities in the distribution of earnings. However, this difference is smaller in Poland than in Hungary[8] (see Table 14). Not only are there larger income differences between the social categories in Poland, but also there are greater economic variations within them than in Hungary. In Hungary there is a wider range between the income extremes ($D_{10} : D_1$) and a higher degree of irregularity characterizes the whole distribution ($M_2 : M_1$). The relative level of income in the bracket above the mean value ($M_2 : M$) is much higher in Hungary than in Poland.

In Hungary there is a particularly marked variability in the distribution of high and low incomes among the households of unskilled and semi-skilled workers. In both countries the degree of variation within the distribution of unskilled and semi-skilled workers is rather similar, but in Poland it is higher in the professional category than in Hungary. The main explanation of the difference between the distribution of earnings and the income-per-person distribution in the two countries derives from differences in demographic features of the household.

TABLE 14
Indices of Irregularity in the Distribution of Income per Person

Social categories	Hungary				Poland			
	$\frac{M_2}{M_1}$	$\frac{M_1}{M}$	$\frac{M_2}{M}$	$\frac{D_{10}}{D_1}$	$\frac{M_2}{M_1}$	$\frac{M_1}{M}$	$\frac{M_2}{M}$	$\frac{D_{10}}{D_1}$
All workers	2.10	0.69	1.45	6.85	1.91	0.71	1.35	4.69
Unskilled workers	2.22	0.67	1.49	8.02	1.92	0.71	1.36	4.84
Skilled workers	1.98	0.70	1.39	5.71	1.94	0.71	1.37	4.73
White-collar workers	1.97	0.72	1.41	6.11	1.74	0.76	1.32	3.37
Professionals	1.96	0.73	1.43	4.84	1.74	0.75	1.30	3.69

Note: The method for calculation of mean measures for income per person is as in Table 11.

In conclusion, it can be observed that the social differentiation of industrial workers' incomes in Hungary and Poland is similar. In Poland these differences are determined to a great extent by classical differences between the social groups, but in Hungary they are the result of a new configuration characterizing the social structure. However, the economic stratification within this configuration makes income distribution more irregular in Hungary than in Poland.

HOUSING

In both countries over 80 percent of respondents (industrial workers) had their own flats — 82 percent in Hungary and 84 percent in Poland. Differences between particular categories were insignificant, but this factor was more marked among white-collar workers. Both countries have a similar living area per person and almost the same density of occupants per flat, but there is a greater difference between the density of the housing of professionals and that of other categories in Poland. There is a greater density of occupants per flat in small towns or in the country but the lowest density pertains to professionals living in small towns.

In both countries there are similar differences between the social categories, with regard to the possession of modern facilities. The housing of unskilled and semi-skilled workers compared with that of professionals contained the following facilities:

Gas
86-98% in Hungary
78-94% in Poland
Running water
72-97% in Hungary
81-97% in Poland
Bathroom
63-95% in Hungary
67-91% in Poland
WC
58-94% in Hungary
71-99% in Poland
Modern heating system
32-60% in Hungary
51-67% in Poland

The data show that, the higher the level of education and the intellectual complexity of work, the better were the modern facilities of the home. The greatest difference between the social categories was in the possession of a telephone. In Hungary only 6 percent and in Poland only 7 percent of unskilled and semi-skilled workers have a telephone, but in Poland the figure is 38 percent for professionals and in Hungary it is 40 percent.

If all aspects of comfort in housing are taken into account, in both countries 33 percent of unskilled and semi-skilled workers, 25 percent of skilled workers, 12 percent of white-collar workers and 6 percent of professionals are living in low-comfort housing. In large cities there are no professionals living in low-comfort housing, and for all other socio-occupational categories, the ratio of those living in low-comfort housing is lower in large cities than in villages (see Table 15). In both countries the situation with regard to low-comfort housing is very similar. In Poland, however, there is a higher ratio of full-comfort housing than low-comfort housing among unskilled and semi-skilled workers compared with skilled workers, but such a ratio does not apply to white-collar workers with secondary education compared with professionals.

TABLE 15
Percentage of Respondents with Fully Comfortable Housing

Social categories	Hungary Total	Hungary Big towns	Poland Total	Poland Big towns
	%	%	%	%
Unskilled workers				
with no subordinates	29	43	39	55
with subordinates	31	50	44	56
Skilled workers				
with no subordinates	38	50	47	59
with subordinates	30	46	57	74
White-collar workers				
with no subordinates	57	72	58	73
with subordinates	61	72	71	82
Professionals				
with no subordinates	76	82	75	80
with subordinates of a higher level	68	74	62	83

To summarize the differences in the housing conditions of each social category, a synthetic index of housing conditions was worked out. The index took into account density, space and housing comfort.[9] The distribution of this index is analysed on the basis of a 9 point scale (similar to the scale of earnings and income). Figure 3 is a graphical presentation of the distribution of dwelling conditions, and Table 16 shows differentials in average values. The analysis of the synthetic index distribution enables one to draw the following conclusions.

1. Although the curves of the housing distribution are very similar in both countries, they are completely different from the income-per-person distribution. In both countries the curves for housing conditions in all the social categories are very highly skewed, as there is a concentration of the population in the top brackets. This means that good housing conditions are typical of industrial workers in both countries.

FIGURE 3
Curves of the Distribution of Housing on the Basis of the Synthetic Index

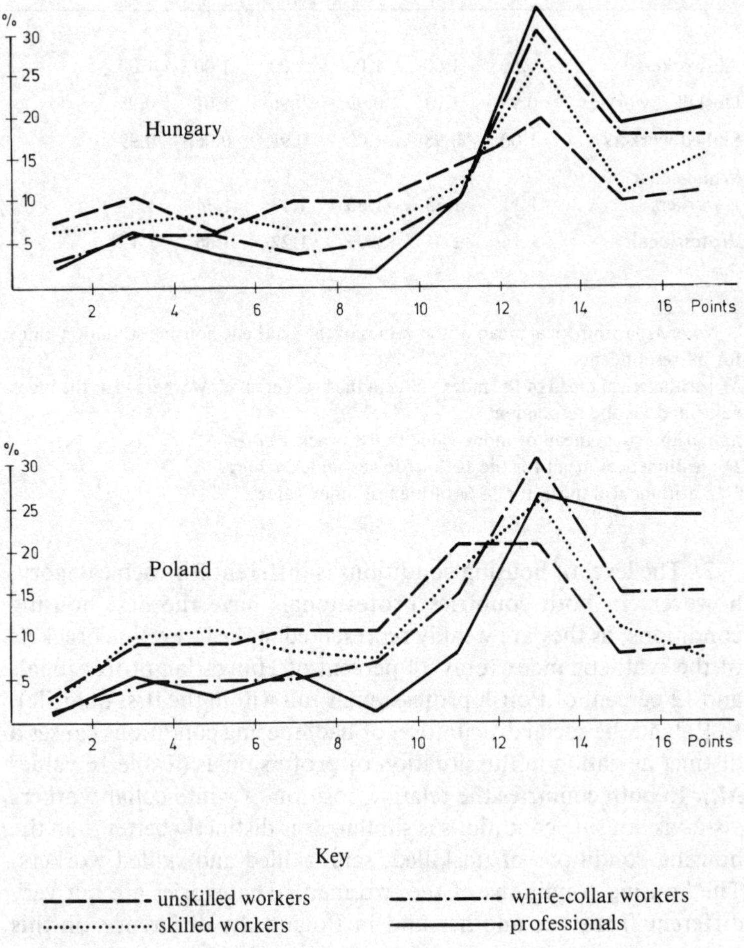

TABLE 16
Range of Housing Levels between Socio-occupational Categories

Social categories	Hungary			Poland		
	M	M_1	M_2	M	M_1	M_2
All workers	1.00	1.00	1.00	1.00	1.00	1.00
Unskilled workers	0.92	1.03	0.99	0.96	1.01	0.98
Skilled workers	1.00	0.98	1.00	0.98	0.96	0.99
White-collar workers	1.11	1.33	1.06	1.13	1.34	1.07
Professionals	1.16	1.31	1.06	1.22	1.66	1.17

Note: M: arithmetical mean of the values of the synthetic housing stituation index for all respondents
M_1: arithmetical mean of the index value in the bracket $m_i < M$ where m_i is the index value and i is the respondent
M_2: arithmetical mean of index value in the bracket $m_i \geqslant \hat{M}$
D_1: arithmetical mean for the 10% of lowest index values
D_{10}: arithmetical mean for 10% of highest index values.

2. The level of housing conditions is different for each category, however. In both countries professionals have the best housing conditions, as they are weakly represented in the low-value brackets of the synthetic index (only 14 percent of Hungarian professionals and 12 percent of Polish professionals fall within the first quartile). In Poland the social distribution of bad housing conditions causes a distinct deviation in the situation of professionals (Table 16 values M_1). In both countries the relative position of white-collar workers vis-à-vis housing conditions is similar. It is distinctly better than the housing conditions of unskilled, semi-skilled and skilled workers. The housing conditions of the two manual categories are not very different from one another and in Poland the differences in this respect are much lower than the differences in income.

3. Differences in the housing conditions of these categories change if the analysis takes into account the worker's actual function. In both countries respondents exercising a managerial

function are less likely to have housing conditions that are below average.

4. Irregularities in the distribution of housing conditions within the social categories are higher in Hungary than in Poland. This is due to the social composition of the below-average bracket (Table 17).

TABLE 17
Indices of Irregularity in the Distribution of Housing Conditions

Social categories	Hungary $\frac{M_2}{M_1}$	$\frac{M_1}{M}$	$\frac{M_2}{M}$	$\frac{D_{10}}{D_1}$	Poland $\frac{M_2}{M_1}$	$\frac{M_1}{M}$	$\frac{M_2}{M}$	$\frac{D_{10}}{D_1}$
All workers	2.45	0.51	1.25	6.39	2.14	1.24	0.58	5.14
Unskilled workers	2.35	0.57	1.34	7.23	2.08	1.27	0.61	5.07
Skilled workers	2.51	0.50	1.26	6.69	2.21	1.26	0.57	4.98
White-collar workers	1.95	0.61	1.19	4.81	1.71	1.18	0.69	3.96
Professionals	1.98	0.58	1.15	4.73	1.51	1.19	0.79	3.83

Note: as in table 16.

A causal analysis of the housing system shows the extent to which its features are explained by household demographic variables, a worker's status and the economic situation of a household. Household demographic features do not account for the difference in housing conditions as much as do other components. In each individual social category demographic features (age, household size and character, number of children) explain 8-14 percent of the variance in housing situation in Poland and 8-19 percent in Hungary. The age factor is most strongly correlated with the housing situation, as it relates to a family's stage in the development cycle. The impact of age on respondent's housing conditions is stronger in Hungary, particularly among white-collar workers.

A closer analysis of the association between the income and the housing situation of industrial workers in Poland and Hungary shows that high values on the two indices are the preserve of certain social groups. A high income per person and good housing conditions are most likely to coincide among white-collar workers and professionals. The coefficients of transition between the highest level on the synthetic index of housing situation (area Q_4) and a high level of income per person (also area Q_4) are shown in Table 18. The data show that low income does not necessarily imply bad housing. Only for one-third of respondents are bad housing conditions matched by low per capita incomes. Low income in professionals' families is not correlated at all with bad housing conditions.

TABLE 18
Coefficients of Transition between the Highest Level on the Synthetic Index of Housing Situation and a High Level of Income per Person

Social categories	Hungary	Poland
All workers	0.52	0.44
Unskilled and semi-skilled workers	0.38	0.35
Skilled workers	0.49	0.35
White-collar workers	0.73	0.57
Professionals	0.60	0.63

In conclusion, we are of the opinion that the factors assessed as potentially accounting for differentials in the global housing conditions of industrial workers are insufficient. The complex character of the phenomenon described by the index increases the set of factors needed to explain the differentials. In both countries, for example, the opportunity for changing a flat is limited. In a statistical picture this fact disturbs the correlations between individual variables. The analysis shows that inequalities in the distribution of housing are determined by various factors that do not run in parallel, such as the social structure and the system of housing itself. Since these indices are not parallel, the housing situation is a vector of their intersection.

HOUSEHOLD EQUIPMENT (CONSUMER DURABLE GOODS)

In analysing the level of household equipment we used as criteria the possession of: a refrigerator, an automatic washing machine, a tape recorder, a stereophonic radio, a ciné-camera, a colour television, a mixer, a sewing machine, a car, a summer house, and a library of more than 100 volumes. We did not take into account a mono-radio set, a black and white television, a bicycle and a camera, on the assumption that such household goods do not illustrate differences in living standards.

The analysis of such household equipment shows that Poland has more of the cheaper consumer durables. In Hungary there are more cars and libraries, and particularly more summer houses. This difference applies to all the social categories.

In both countries the relative scale proposed by Zdrawomysłow was used in order to avoid the imposition of a pre-conceived consumption model on the different populations. A synthetic index of equipment was calculated for each country, and individual objects were ranked according to the intensity of a given need for them (based on the percentage of people who do not possess a given thing). The synthetic index measured the extent to which needs for domestic equipment were satisfied in relation to average consumption in a given country. Points obtained by individual respondents were distributed on a 9 point scale.

The distribution of consumer durable goods and the factors that explain the irregularity of their distribution were then analysed. In Poland and Hungary the differences in their distribution between each social category are similar (see Table 19). A striking feature is the really substantial difference between the households of unskilled and semi-skilled workers (particularly in Hungary) compared with the well-equipped homes of professionals. In the graphic representation of the distributions (Figure 4) the curves for these two categories are characterized by reverse forms of asymmetry, skewed to the right for professionals and to the left for unskilled and semi-skilled workers. The general configuration is similar in both countries, but in Poland the white-collar category (those with secondary education) is much closer to the professional category. In both countries, therefore, household equipment is the most highly differentiated component of living conditions.

TABLE 19
Range of Household Equipment between Social Categories

	Hungary			Poland		
Social categories	*M*	M_1	M_2	*M*	M_1	M_2
All workers	1.00	1.00	1.00	1.00	1.00	1.00
Unskilled workers	0.73	0.60	0.74	0.80	0.79	0.84
Skilled workers	1.05	1.14	1.00	1.06	1.16	1.04
White-collar workers	1.28	1.50	1.16	1.42	1.80	1.31
Professionals	1.58	2.14	1.35	1.68	2.16	1.43

Note: M: arithmetical mean of the equipment synthetic value for all respondents
M_1: arithmetical mean of the index value in the bracket $m_i < M$ where m_i is index value and *i* is the respondent
M_2: arithmetical mean of index in the bracket $m_1 \geqslant \hat{M}$
D_1: arithmetical mean for the 10% of lowest index values
D_{10}: arithmetical mean for the 10% of highest index values.

The relatively strong impact of membership of a particular social category is shown by the fact that in both countries approximately one-third of unskilled and semi-skilled workers, one-fifth of skilled workers, one-eighth of white-collar workers and only one-tenth of professionals have badly equipped households (points 1 and 2 on the scale). Conversely, in both Poland and Hungary half of the professionals, one-third of the white-collar workers, one-fourth of skilled workers and one-tenth of unskilled and semi-skilled workers have homes that are extremely well equipped (6 to 9 points on the scale). However, in each social category the level of equipment varies according to occupational position.

An analysis of two very fundamental demographic features — belonging to a socio-occupational category and having a permanent address — showed that they accounted for 17 percent of the recorded variance on the index of equipment in each social category. Once again, key aspects of the social structure have the strongest effect in this area. The correlation between the level of income and the level of equipment was analysed because of the

FIGURE 4
Curves of the Distribution of Equipment on the Basis of the Synthetic Index

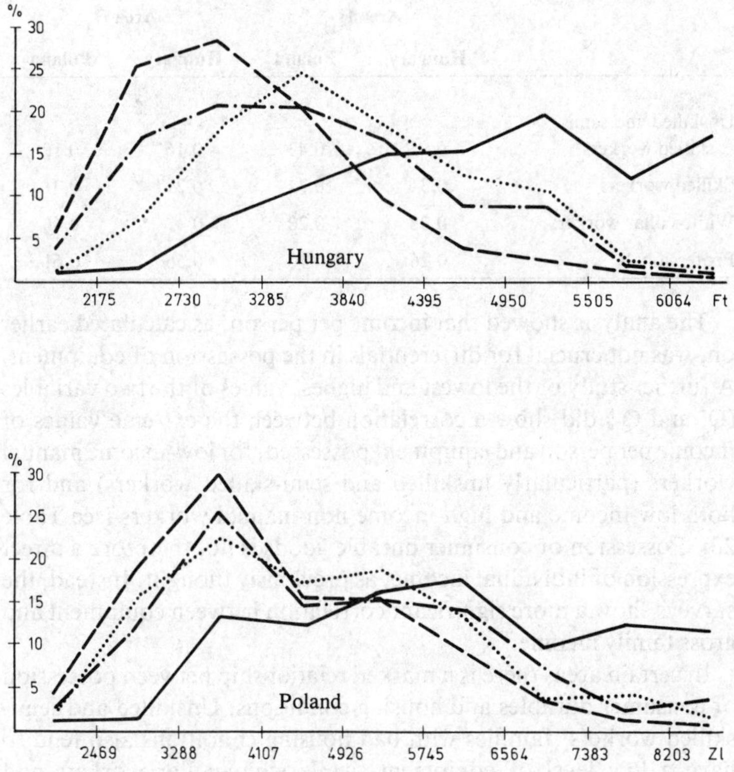

Key

- – – – – unskilled workers
- ············ skilled workers
- –·–·–·– white-collar workers
- ———— professionals

particularly sharp differences of equipment levels and the depth of the plunge registered among the section falling below the average.

TABLE 20
Correlation between the Extreme Values of Income per Person and Equipment Possessed

	Area Q_1		Area Q_4	
	Hungary	Poland	Hungary	Poland
Unskilled and semi-skilled workers	0.05	0.43	0.16	0.19
Skilled workers	0.31	0.34	0.27	0.31
White-collar workers	0.28	0.20	0.42	0.46
Professionals	0.26	0.10	0.56	0.61

The analysis showed that income per person, as calculated earlier on, was not crucial for differentials in the possession of equipment. A further study of the lowest and highest values of the two variables (Q_1 and Q_4) did show a correlation between the extreme values of income per person and equipment possessed, for low-income manual workers (particularly unskilled and semi-skilled workers) and for both low-income and high-income non-manual workers (see Table 20). Possession of consumer durable goods is not therefore a direct expression of individual income, as previously thought. Instead, the surveys show a more significant correlation between equipment and gross family income.

In certain areas there is a marked relationship between possession of consumer durables and housing conditions. Unskilled and semi-skilled workers' families with bad housing conditions also tend to have a low level of equipment, while white-collar workers and professionals with good housing conditions tend to enjoy a high level of equipment. Coefficients of transition are shown in Table 22. It seems that the presence of such strong differentiation in terms of household equipment is a two-sided problem.

1. To a certain extent, it is due to the cumulation of negative factors contributing to a low standard of living among unskilled and semi-skilled workers (low income per person plus bad housing conditions plus a low level of domestic equipment), and of positive

factors contributing to a high standard of living among professionals and white-collar workers.

TABLE 21
Indices of Irregularity in Equipment with Consumer Durables

Social categories	Hungary				Poland			
	$\frac{M_2}{M_1}$	$\frac{M_1}{M}$	$\frac{M_2}{M}$	$\frac{D_{10}}{D_1}$	$\frac{M_2}{M_1}$	$\frac{M_1}{M}$	$\frac{M_2}{M}$	$\frac{D_{10}}{D_1}$
All workers	3.65	0.46	1.68	62.3	3.62	0.55	1.62	78.3
Unskilled workers	4.51	0.38	1.71	139.0	3.85	0.44	1.69	99.3
Skilled workers	3.21	0.50	1.61	48.1	3.25	0.49	1.59	63.2
White-collar workers	2.82	0.54	1.52	23.4	2.63	0.57	1.50	14.4
Professionals	2.31	0.62	1.43	9.9	2.40	0.58	1.39	11.4

Note: as in table 19.

TABLE 22
Coefficients of Transition between Possession of Consumer Durables and Housing Conditions

	Area Q_1		Area Q_4	
	Hungary	Poland	Hungary	Poland
Unskilled and semi-skilled workers	0.58	0.56	0.17	0.20
Skilled workers	0.31	0.41	0.28	0.38
White-collar workers	0.25	0.19	0.45	0.44
Professionals	0.17	0.25	0.60	0.60

2. However, there is also a cultural component influencing different consumption patterns, and thus non-economic factors have a strong impact on consumption preferences.

LIVING CONDITIONS AND THEIR IMPACT ON SOCIAL STRATIFICATION

The analysis of the correlation between individual components of living conditions has shown that respondents' earnings have an insignificant effect on other components. However, a family's standard of life is affected by such factors as the earnings of other household members, welfare allowances received, number of children and the occupational activity of the household members. Therefore general household income and income per person are directly correlated with living conditions. Further analysis took into account income per person as a component of living conditions, and Table 23 shows a comprehensive picture of the relationships between components investigated.

TABLE 23
Coefficients of Correlation (*r*) between Components of Living Conditions

Social categories	Income × housing situation		Income × household equipment		Household equipment × housing situation	
	Hungary	Poland	Hungary	Poland	Hungary	Poland
All workers	0.24	0.25	0.12	0.24	0.23	0.31
Unskilled workers	0.17	0.23	0.03	0.18	0.21	0.32
Skilled workers	0.24	0.12	0.12	0.14	0.15	0.30
White-collar workers	0.33	0.36	0.13	0.21	0.19	0.17
Professionals	0.23	0.25	0.10	0.18	0.17	0.34

In both Hungary and Poland there is a weak correlation between particular components of individual industrial workers' living conditions and between components determining the living conditions of each social category. In Poland there is a significant correlation between household equipment and the housing situation, and income has a greater impact on household equipment

ment than in Hungary. In both countries there is a relatively strong correlation ($r = 0.4$) between the density of flats and income per person and between the level of equipment (comfort in housing) and the gross household income.

TABLE 24
Coefficients of Transition in Three-dimensional Space (Income per Person, Equipment with Consumer Durables, Housing Conditions in General)

	Q_1		Q_2		Q_3		Q_4	
Social categories	**Hungary**	**Poland**	**Hungary**	**Poland**	**Hungary**	**Poland**	**Hungary**	**Poland**
All workers	0.15	0.18	0.05	0.08	0.08	0.09	0.20	0.23
Unskilled workers	0.21	0.22	0.08	0.09	0.07	0.07	0.06	0.10
Skilled workers	0.09	0.16	0.04	0.11	0.06	0.10	0.15	0.16
White-collar workers	0.08	0.07	0.03	0.05	0.08	0.09	0.35	0.28
Professionals	0.07	0.05	0.09	0.04	0.10	0.13	0.34	0.39

As non-linear correlations were not calculated, the correlation coefficients presented may not adequately reflect the association between the various components of living conditions for certain categories. An attempt to explain the correlations detected was also made by use of factor analysis (VARIMAX type of rotation using SPSS). As results of the factor analysis are connected with the number and structure of the variables analysed, it was carried out in two ways, first using the set of aggregate indices and second employing primary information (which makes up the aggregate indices).

The basic results of the factor analysis were as follows.

1. In both countries the differentiation of living conditions is best reflected by housing conditions, and the density of occupants per flat in particular.

2. In both countries the density of occupants per flat and the level of income per person have a similar effect on differentiation in living conditions.

3. In both countries there is a strong correlation between the level of domestic equipment and level of comfort in housing.

4. Possession of a telephone is correlated with possession of consumer durable goods but not with level of comfort. Possession of a refrigerator is correlated with the possession of a flat or house, but not with owning other domestic equipment.

5. Respondent's earnings have an indirect and *almost* imperceptible effect on the differentiation of living conditions in Poland and Hungary.

6. Among factors indicative of domestic comfort, the strongest correlation with other factors is the possession of a bathroom and WC.

7. In Poland the level of household equipment makes a stronger contribution to the differentiation of living conditions than in Hungary.

8. In Hungary the level of household equipment is determined by the possession of a colour TV set, a ciné-camera, a stereophonic radio set and a summer house, but in Poland the possession of a car is the most strongly determining factor. The factors determining the level of household equipment are also those most closely connected with the global differentiation of living conditions.

9. The possession of a flat/house contributes more to the differentiation of living conditions in Poland than in Hungary.

In the analysis synthesizing the individual components of living conditions we attempted to construct a comprehensive index. The index included income per person, a synthetic measure of equipment with consumer durable goods, and leisure time in days off work. As all these components are measured by 9 point scales, the comprehensive index is calculated by adding together the points obtained by a respondent on all the scales. This synthesized index of living conditions thus has a range of from 4 to 36 points.

The drawback of this comprehensive index is that it attaches the same importance to all components of living conditions. It must also be taken into consideration that the concept of rest or leisure-time was differently understood in the two countries. However, the data show a strong correlation between the components (0.53-0.67). In Hungary membership of a particular socio-occupational category (r = 0.34) and in Poland the possession of a permanent address (r = 0.31) are the most strongly differentiating variables. Considered in toto,

FIGURE 5
Curves of the Distribution of Living Conditions on the Basis of the Synthetic Index

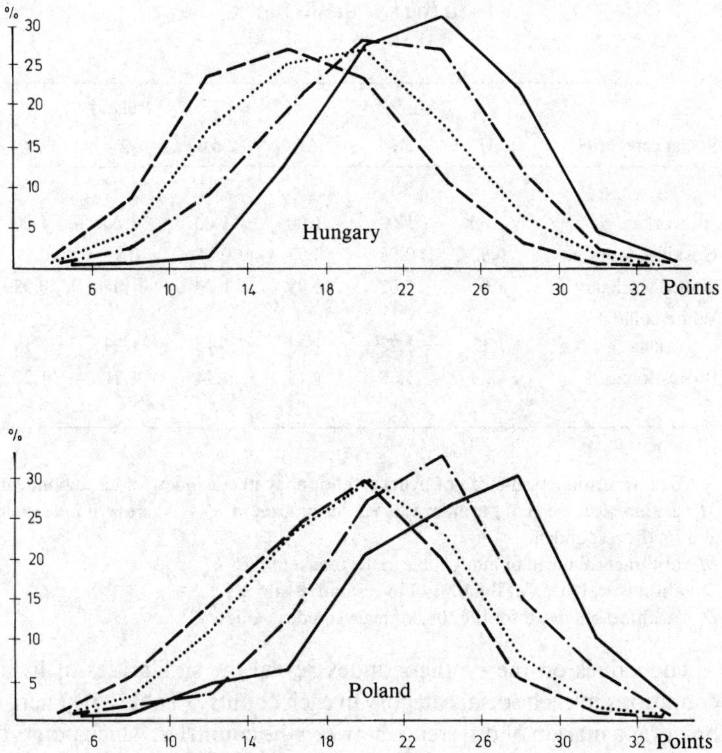

Key

unskilled workers — white-collar workers

skilled workers — professionals

demographic variables, socio-occupational categories and a permanent address explain 24 percent of variance in the index scores. Variation in living conditions in different socio-occupational categories is due to many factors.

TABLE 25
Range of Living Conditions According to the Synthetic Index

	Hungary			Poland		
Social categories	M	M_1	M_2	M	M_1	M_2
All workers	1.00	1.00	1.00	1.00	1.00	1.00
Unskilled workers	0.90	0.98	0.97	0.95	0.99	0.97
Skilled workers	1.01	1.02	0.99	1.00	1.01	0.98
White-collar workers	1.12	1.28	1.13	1.15	1.29	1.13
Professionals	1.24	1.38	1.15	1.24	1.51	1.27

Note: M: arithmetical mean of living conditions synthetic index for all respondents
M_1: arithmetical mean of the index value in the bracket $m_i < M$ where m_i is index value and i is the respondent
M_2: arithmetical mean of index value in the bracket $m_1 \geqslant \hat{M}$
D_1: arithmetical mean of the 10% of lowest index values
D_{10}: arithmetical mean for the 10% of highest index values.

The values on the synthetic index reveal the similarities of living conditions in each social category in each country (Table 25). There is however a margin of difference between the countries, which points to certain nuances in the social structure affecting the distribution of living conditions. In Hungary the average situation of unskilled workers is further below the mean than in Poland. The relative (i.e., compared with the average value for all categories) level of skilled workers' earnings is the same in Poland and Hungary. The difference in the position of unskilled and semi-skilled workers means that in Hungary skilled workers are placed exactly between unskilled workers on the one hand and professionals on the other. In contrast to Poland, every jump in social category is characterized by the 11-12 percent increase in the level of living conditions. In Poland the global living conditions of unskilled and semi-skilled workers are weakly differentiated but white-collar workers with secondary education are closer to professionals and further away from skilled workers than in Hungary. In Poland the living standards of unskilled and semi-skilled workers approach one another, as do those of white-collar workers and professionals, but there is a significant difference between non-manual and manual workers.

TABLE 26
Indices of Irregularity in the Distribution of Living Conditions, According to the Synthetic Index

Social categories	Hungary				Poland			
	$\frac{M_2}{M_1}$	$\frac{M_1}{M}$	$\frac{M_2}{M}$	$\frac{D_{10}}{D_1}$	$\frac{M_2}{M_1}$	$\frac{M_1}{M}$	$\frac{M_2}{M}$	$\frac{D_{10}}{D_1}$
All workers	1.70	0.73	2.33	3.05	1.68	0.70	2.40	2.97
Unskilled workers	1.69	0.78	2.17	3.46	1.66	0.73	2.27	2.94
Skilled workers	1.65	0.73	2.26	2.80	1.63	0.71	2.30	2.77
White-collar workers	1.50	0.82	1.83	2.60	1.47	0.79	1.86	2.40
Professionals	1.43	0.79	1.81	2.05	1.42	0.85	1.67	2.39

Note: as in Table 23.

Turning to the internal distribution of the comprehensive index for each social category, the graphic presentation of its distributive curves (Figure 5) and the measures of distributional irregularity (Table 26) show the global situation to be even more pronounced because of the cumulation of various levels of the components of living conditions within the social categories. In both countries the curves representing living conditions among unskilled, semi-skilled and skilled workers assume the shape of a normal distribution but the curves for professionals and white-collar workers with secondary education in Poland (this is less distinct in Hungary) are skewed towards the higher values. Overall this signifies that social category exerts a very small force in the low brackets of values on the synthetic index but a stronger one in the average and high brackets. In both countries the general irregularity in the distribution of living conditions is smaller than that of each component (Table 27).

TABLE 27
Coefficients of Deviation from Proportional Representation in the Distribution of the Components of Living Conditions Investigated (on the Basis of Synthetic Index)

Social categories	Low level		Middle level		High level	
	Hungary	Poland	Hungary	Poland	Hungary	Poland
Unskilled workers						
with no subordinates	1.46	1.37	0.92	0.98	0.43	0.54
with subordinates	1.16	0.69	0.97	1.07	0.55	1.04
Skilled workers						
with no subordinates	1.00	1.10	1.03	1.04	0.76	0.71
with subordinates	0.74	0.74	1.04	1.09	1.39	0.95
White-collar workers						
with no subordinates	0.58	0.38	1.08	1.00	1.59	1.97
with subordinates	0.32	0.21	1.15	1.00	1.58	2.32
Professionals						
with no subordinates	0.35	0.68	0.96	0.84	3.00	2.64
with subordinates of higher level	0.05	—	1.07	0.65	3.00	4.82

We can conclude that in both countries the living conditions of 70 percent of the industrial workers are at an average level (15-25 points). Differences between categories are insignificant except for professionals in Poland. Differences between the social categories are of course connected with the degree to which workers are concentrated in the low- and high-value brackets. In both countries a deeper analysis of the low- and high-value brackets shows that a worker's function produces clearly marked differences; for example, managerial functions increase the chance of achieving better living conditions (see Table 28).

To sum up our results, we would like to emphasize that the method used only analysed the *relative situation* of the social categories as regards living conditions in a given country, and provided a comparison of the two countries. The results of the investigation do not provide the basis for a comparison of the actual level of living conditions in individual social categories in each country.

TABLE 28
Percentage of Workers Living in Different Conditions

Social categories	Low level		Middle level		High level	
	Hungary	Poland	Hungary	Poland	Hungary	Poland
	%	%	%	%	%	%
All workers	22	14	68	72	10	14
Unskilled workers	34	21	62	73	4	6
Skilled workers	22	15	70	76	8	9
White-collar workers	12	6	74	72	14	22
Professionals	3	5	70	63	27	32

CONCLUSIONS

The following general conclusions can be drawn from the investigations.

1. There are more similarities than differences in the living conditions of industrial workers in Poland and Hungary. There is the same variation between social categories with regard to housing conditions and possession of durable consumer goods. In Poland there is greater social differentiation in terms of income-per-person distribution. In Hungary there is a higher degree of economic stratification within the social categories, particularly among unskilled and semi-skilled workers.

2. In both countries a similar distance separates unskilled and semi-skilled workers from professionals as regards living conditions. However, qualitatively different phenomena in fact underlie this similarity. In Hungary the distance between the two categories is due to the fact that unskilled workers fall below the average level, whereas in Poland this derives from the professionals being above the average level.

3. In both countries there is a different relationship between the general living conditions (and their various components) of skilled

workers and white-collar workers with secondary education. In Hungary these categories are less differentiated than in Poland.

4. In Hungary there is a greater distance between unskilled, semi-skilled and skilled workers as well as between professionals and white-collar workers, while in Poland there is a greater distance between professionals and skilled workers.

5. The analysis shows that in Poland differences between manual and non-manual workers' living conditions are greater than in Hungary. In Hungary three different patterns of living standards can be distinguished: those of (1) unskilled and semi-skilled workers, (2) skilled workers and white-collar workers and (3) professionals. In Poland such patterns as are found are more reflective of the traditional class structure, while the Hungarian picture mirrors to a greater extent the emergence of new factors in the social structure.

6. Our investigation proved that in both countries there is stratification of material living conditions. It is levelled by some factors, such as the distribution of flats and welfare fund payments. The levelling impact of these factors, however, is not complete and is not always positive. Instead, demographic features exert the strongest influence on the living conditions of household members.

The following general conclusion can be drawn from the foregoing review of factors that determine the living conditions of the families of industrial workers — and this includes the impact of demographic features. *Inequalities in material living conditions, as observed in both countries, are due to unequal chances of attaining a specific living standard and not to planned systems of distribution.* Thus, although not all professionals live in better conditions, their chances in this respect are better than those of workers in other categories.

NOTES

1. New research findings show that salaries/wages are a determinant not only of economic but also of social status. This tendency is supported by our investigations. See Claus Offe, *Leistungsprinzip und Industrielle Arbeit*, Frankfurt am Main, 1970; Pierre Ranval, *Hierarchie des saliers et lutte des classes*, Paris, 1972.

2. Coefficient of multiple correlation between a set of variables and one variable on the basis of regression analysis.

3. Detailed investigations carried out in Hungary concerning the distribution of workers' earnings show that with 22 variables introduced into the regression analysis, 70 percent of the variance in earnings could be accounted for. See *Uj módszer a fizikai dolgozók berarányainak vizsagálatára* (A New Method of Analysis of Manual Workers' Wage Structure). Budapest, 1979, KSU.

4. See S. Ferge, E. Silk, E. Havasi, A. Horváth and J. Szalai, 'A társadalompolitika, a jovedelempolitika és a társadalmi struktura', in *Társadalmi strukturánk fejlödése* (The Development of our Social Structure), Vol. 3, Budapest, 1978.

5. Detailed investigations carried out in Poland and Hungary reveal that these variables do not act directly but through the indirect influence they exert, e.g., the extent that occupationally active persons are burdened with members of the inactive population. See Ferge et al., op. cit.; and L. Beskid, *Konsumpcja w rodzinach pracowniczych* (Consumption in Labourers' Families), Warsaw, 1977, pp. 75-91.

6. Investigations carried out in Poland show that white-collar workers in certain professions aim at reaching a higher consumption level at the cost of smaller families and more work. See J. Sikorska, *Społeczno-ekonomiczne zróżnicowanie wzorów konsumpcji* (Socio-economic Differentiation of Consumption Patterns in Labourers' Households), Warsaw, 1979, s. 86. Hungarian investigations show that a large number of children is a more serious problem for manual workers than for non-manual workers. For instance, the income per person in three-children families constitutes 45 percent of the income per person in childless manual workers' families. The same proportion for white-collar families is 53 percent (see Ferge et al., op. cit., p. 30).

7. The level of income (as for earnings) was determined on the basis of a 9 point scale. The scale is limited by the mean value points for the first and tenth deciles — low income was taken to be represented by point 2 on the scale and high income by point 8.

8. The investigation of inequality in the distribution of earnings and income per person for all workers employed in the Polish nationalized economy point to the almost identical degrees of differentiation in the two distributions: see *Income Differences of Working People in Poland*, Oeconomica Polana, 1978, no. 2. There is a similar situation in Hungary. Income differentiation for the whole population according to $D_{10} : D_1$ is more than fourfold. However, if estimates derived from the secondary economy (extra income from various sources) are taken into account, then the difference increases to six or to eightfold.

9. For details about the methodology employed in the construction of the indices, see Tamás Kolosi, 'Special programme on the analysis of the material conditions of life' (in manuscript).

4

PATTERNS OF LEISURE

Edmund Wnuk-Lipiński

The first part of this chapter deals with cultural activity and the second with the way people spend their paid holidays.

If approached comparatively, the analysis of cultural activity is complex, and if doubts expressed by sociologists of culture[1] were to be taken into account, a separate analysis of the problem of cultural participation in the two countries would be called for. In this survey we reconstructed selected features of cultural activity among industrial workers in Poland and Hungary on the basis of certain quantitative indices, and we were limited by many of the shortcomings of quantitative investigations into cultural participation.[2] However, a purely qualitative approach also has shortcomings,[3] and they are particularly significant in comparative study.

The social goal of bringing manual and non-manual workers closer together exhibits different rates of success in relation to social differentiation (living standards, conditions of work, social activity, participation in cultural pursuits, etc). In some of these areas the target is more closely approached than in others, but there is also the emergence of social inequalities owing to the changing conditions in Polish and Hungarian society to take into account. The processes of the first type can be called 'de-structuralization', i.e., the obliteration of social differences, and the second type 're-structuralization', the forming of new types of differentiation.[4] From the theoretical point of view, these 'new' differences can be two-sided — they may simply be a reproduction of the social structures of the past, or they can represent an entirely new phenomenon.

The reproduction of various dimensions of social differentiation is a result of two different aspects of social mobility: either a person's social status differs from his or her father's on one or more levels (education, place in the power structure, standard of living, etc.), or else 'inheritance of social status' occurs when father and child have the same position in the social hierarchy. The reproduction of professionals, or of manual workers, takes place not only because successive generations remain in the same social category, but also because of the intake from other social categories.

How much do these complex processes of de-structuralization and re-structuralization affect the recognized patterns of leisure and cultural activity? Some specialists (e.g. Bourdieu[5]) tend to stick to the thesis that the reproduction of cultural participation is secondary to the reproduction of the social structure, as the latter is of importance in determining cultural values. Others are of the opinion that cultural activities are to some extent an autonomous phenomenon in relation to the social structure, as there are certain categories of people who are homogeneous in terms of cultural activity yet belong to different social categories.[6]

Empirical evidence shows that there is a clear correlation between primary indices of cultural activity and membership of different social categories, although there is a slightly stronger correlation in Hungary than in Poland.

For the purposes of this analysis we assumed that the processes in the course of which social differentiation in the sphere of cultural and leisure activity either disappear or are reproduced take place on two planes:

1. actual behaviour
2. aspirations.

Our investigation of cultural activity and spare time had (1) a descriptive objective — what form does participation in chosen types of cultural and leisure activity assume in Hungary and Poland? — and (2) an explanatory objective — why did participation assume this particular form?

CULTURAL ACTIVITY

If cultural activity is analysed in terms of distances between manual and non-manual workers, the notion of distance must be defined. Terms such as 'cultural advancement', 'inequalities' and 'cultural backwardness' are connected with an implicit vertical concept of cultural participation. 'Cultural advancement' means passing from the lower to the upper level of participation; 'backwardness' is a euphemistic term describing a negative evaluation of 'low-level' cultural activity (from the point of its view of frequency, quality or both). There has been debate for years over whether it is correct to apply such evaluative notions to cultural participation. Both quantitative and qualitative criteria contain a certain element of arbitrariness, and are not always clearly defined either.

However, the terms continue to be used, as all the concepts of egalitarianization and democratization in relation to culture are based on the vertical concept of cultural participation. The opposite assumption would imply that all attempts at the democratization of culture would be meaningless because all participation levels would be equally 'good' (including the lack of any participation in the institutionalized transmission of cultural values). A more general consideration, although perhaps not so easily accepted by methodological purists, has emerged from reference to the attitudes of actors themselves. In Europe, cultural participation is commonly perceived hierarchically. European civilization has produced different institutions with varying levels of difficulty and varying social functions — for example, different functions are fulfilled by a circus and the Philharmonic Orchestra. No participation at all is felt to be something 'worse' than an elementary-level participation. Thus, respondents often over-estimate their degree of cultural activity as the cultural participation of higher-status groups is usually perceived by the lower-status category as the model for social advancement. However, the vertical concept of cultural participation is particularly frequent among people who move upwards culturally, and appears less often among people characterized by a stable pattern in the cultural domain. Z. Bokszański states:

> Among people who advance, the expression of internal divisions within symbolic culture shows aesthetic evaluation, or is connected with social stratification. As a result 'advancing' people more frequently picture culture in terms of vertical divisions than do stable people. It can be assumed that this way of looking at culture is very important for the understanding of the social environment, and it functions as a significant criterion of choice. There is a comparison of personal standards with standards at 'higher' and 'lower' levels, comparisons which are important in the cultural advancement process. The investigation shows that more than a half of the people who advance, compared to one-fifth of stable people, have a concept of culture that made advancement meaningful.[7]

(This is drawn from a discussion of research findings on the cultural activity of young workers.)

The adoption of a vertical concept of cultural activity makes it possible to use such terms as 'cultural mobility', 'cultural advancement' and 'cultural degradation'.

For the purpose of our survey, only quantitative criteria of cultural activity were taken into account, and qualitative aspects were regarded as being of secondary importance. Even in studies of cultural participation confined to one country, consideration of qualitative aspects means confronting formidable methodological difficulties, and these become almost insuperable in international comparative research.

Model 1: TV-viewers

Earlier investigations carried out in both countries show that television, as a mass medium transmitting culture, has exhibited the highest rate of development.

Time budget analyses conducted in Poland in 1969 and 1976 proved that watching television is a prevalent activity not only during the week (spare time during the day) but also on days off. It consumes almost half the spare time of occupationally active people.[8] The results of Hungarian investigations were very similar.[9]

Television has been the cause of numerous controversies among cultural specialists, and there are two extreme attitudes expressed. On the one hand, television is said to be a powerful medium for cultural democratization, and its diversified programmes meet the demands of a large audience which otherwise would not have such a broad contact with a range of cultural values. Apart from providing entertainment, television plays an important part in breaking up the spatial and social barriers that bar access to culture. In many cases it is the only channel that provides those social categories, which are often described as backward in their cultural development, with any cultural values at all.

On the other hand, television is often blamed for promoting a uniform view of the world, for substituting an inauthentic and indirect contact with culture, and for a gradual and imperceptible replacement of the civilization based on 'printing' by a civilization of 'pictures'. The detractors of television say that it is too verbatim in nature to leave room for the development of imagination, particularly where children and young people are concerned.

We consider such arguments to be a good starting point for the analysis of the comparative data collected in Poland and Hungary.

TABLE 1
Frequency of Television-viewing by the Industrial Workers in Both Countries

	Poland	Hungary
	%	%
Every day	74.6	83.4
Less frequently	24.8	15.1
Not at all	0.6	1.5

Table 1 shows that in both Poland and Hungary television-viewing is a daily occurrence among the majority of industrial workers. In Hungary the percentage of people who watch television is somewhat higher. However, although fewer people watch television every day in Poland than in Hungary, the total amount of time spent watching television is greater in Poland (see Table 2).

TABLE 2
Amount of Time Spent Watching Television Every Day

	Poland	Hungary
	%	%
Up to two hours	27.1	43.6
From 2 to 4 hours	59.4	46.5
More than 4 hours	13.5	9.9

At first sight this widespread viewing pattern seems to justify those humanists who foresee that television (the reception of which is relatively easy) will gradually replace other kinds of cultural activity. However, the question of whether television replaces other cultural activities or is rather a preliminary stage in cultural initiation — that is, whether it encourages people to go to the theatre, opera, cinema, see an exhibition or listen to a concert — remains open. If television is competing with other kinds of cultural activity without being branded in advance as a substitute for them, then, it is reasonable to expect that it would enjoy equal popularity among the culturally more advanced social categories and those social groups whose pattern of cultural activity is less rich. However, data point to a somewhat different phenomenon.

TABLE 3
Frequency of Television-viewing among Manual and Non-manual Workers in Poland and Hungary

Frequency of television-viewing	Unskilled workers	Skilled workers	White-collar workers	Profes-sionals
	%	%	%	%
Poland				
Total	100.0	100.0	100.0	100.0
Every day	74.3	73.7	78.6	63.9
Less frequently	24.8	26.2	21.2	35.4
Not at all	0.9	0.1	0.2	0.7
	(*N* = 968)	(*N* = 675)	(*N* = 412)	(*N* = 294)
Hungary				
Total	100.0	100.0	100.0	100.0
Every day	84.4	82.7	86.2	71.7
Less frequently	13.5	16.2	12.5	27.6
Not at all	2.1	1.1	1.3	0.7
	(*N* = 822)	(*N* = 645)	(*N* = 382)	(*N* = 301)

In both countries professionals are less attracted to television than are workers in the other three social categories, which are practically identical in their viewing frequency (see Table 3). It is possible that for professionals, television is but one of the components of a richer and more diversified pattern of cultural activity, while for other social categories it frequently substitutes for any other cultural activity. If television really is replacing other kinds of culture, the process is least advanced among professionals.

However, the question of whether, in Poland and Hungary, there are social groups for whom television is practically the only medium transmitting culture remains open. The existence of such groups would support the thesis that television is replacing other cultural activities, at least for a certain part of the population.

A synthetic index was worked out to test this thesis and to define the size and distribution of the population geared towards television. Only those people were included who watch television every day, and who generally do not read books, go to the theatre, cinema, opera, museums, concerts, circus, sports matches or visit exhibitions. Although it is a simplification, the term 'television type' of cultural participation (i.e., an institutionalized form of receiving cultural values) is used for this category.

TABLE 4
Percentage of Respondents with a 'Television Type' of Cultural Participation

	Hungary	Poland
Unskilled workers	27	23
Skilled workers	11	11
White-collar workers	10	7
Professionals	2	4
Total	17	10

It is characteristic that in Poland and Hungary the proportion of 'television-type' cultural participants is similar (for 16 percent of all respondents television is the only institutionalized medium of culture). This specific type of participation varies according to socio-occupational category (see Table 4). As the social categories get higher, there is a marked decrease in the percentage of respondents for whom television is the only medium transmitting cultural values.

It can be concluded from the data that the confinement of cultural participation to the most popular medium is, in both countries, conditioned by the social category of the respondent.

In both Hungary and Poland social categories are correlated with educational level: education is therefore a differentiating factor. The ratio of 'television types', not surprisingly, is found to differ according to education[10] (see Table 5). It can be concluded that a lower social category is usually accompanied by a lower educational level, which implies a poorer pattern of cultural participation. Therefore, the thesis may be ventured that, the lower the education level, the greater the number of 'television types' among cultural participants.

TABLE 5
Correlation of Television-viewing Habits with Educational Background

	Hungary	Poland
	%	%
Elementary level of education	28	22
Secondary level	9	11
University	2	6

The aim of our survey is to extend these conclusions by investigating the whole process of participating in institutionalized forms of cultural transmission.

If cultural participation is discussed in a dynamic context, the reproduction of patterns from generation to generation would result from the interaction of numerous more or less important factors. One of the simplest, and at the same time most simplified, assumptions can be formulated as follows.

What constitutes the basic criterion of cultural advancement for people in the low socio-occupational status families with a low educational level is generally the pattern of cultural participation of people in higher social status families.

The adoption of this assumption is not without certain consequences, as is emphasized by R. Boudon.[11] Apart from the phenomenon described as 'advancement', any vertical concept of cultural mobility also entails the phenomena described as 'degradation'.

Boudon has observed that people of 'high-status' origin are less likely to advance culturally than people of 'low-status' origin, but are also in greater danger of cultural degradation. Consideration of the fact that these two groups have different reference points for the assessment of their participation in terms of advancement and degradation makes this more subjectively meaningful. For people in high socio-occupational status families the preservation of the same level of cultural participation is no advancement but is merely the reproduction of the cultural pattern of the home. For people in families of low socio-occupational status groups, the prospect of cultural advancement is greater, as the assessment of their cultural activity (the pattern of home culture) is too low to be threatened with degradation.

Therefore, people of 'high-status' origin may be expected to exhibit a relatively strong tendency towards inter-generational reproduction of cultural participation patterns, while people of 'low-status' origin are likely to exhibit a relatively strong inclination to change their cultural participation patterns.

When the quantitative aspect is taken into account, it may be assumed that cultural advancement exhibits, among other things, a greater number of cultural activities. The data in Table 6 reveal certain points related to television. These data show that the situation in Poland is a little different from that in Hungary. In Hungary the respondent's father's education and, indirectly, the home have an impact only on those respondents with an elementary education. In this group respondents whose fathers are better educated pursue the 'television type' of cultural participation less frequently than do respondents with the same educational level as their fathers, but in other groups there are no significant dependencies of this kind.

In Poland the education of the respondent's father has an impact on all respondents despite differing levels of education but the percentage is higher where the 'television type' of cultural participation is concerned among respondents whose fathers have a low level of education.

In both countries, therefore, the percentage of respondents with a 'television type' of culture is highest among respondents whose fathers have had a low level of education. However, such respondents were mostly older people, as the investigation showed that young people are much less frequently satisfied with television as the only form of cultural activity.

TABLE 6
Respondents with only the 'Television-type' of Cultural Participation, According to Relationship between Respondent's and Father's Education

	Respondent's educational level						
	Elementary		Secondary			University	
	Higher than father's	Same as father's	Higher than father's	Same as father's	Lower than father's	Same as father's	Lower than father's
	%	%	%	%	%	%	%
Poland	19.4	22.6	6.2	6.5	13.5	1.3	6.4
Hungary	16.3	30.2	10.0	5.6	10.3	2.5	1.7

The percentage of people below 30 who pursue the 'television type' of cultural participation is 11 percent in Hungary and 10 percent in Poland; in both countries the percentage of such people between 31 and 44 is 16 percent, and the percentage of such people over 45 is 24 percent in Hungary and 23 percent in Poland. Such results can be accounted for by the fact that in both countries older people are less educated, and that young people prefer other forms of cultural participation.

Model 2: Book Readership

The analysis of readership habits shows that both the kind of books and the frequency with which they are read are affected by other cultural activities, and that reading habits also determine the forms and content of other types of cultural participation.[12] Certain writers are of the opinion that reading habits occupy a special position among different forms of cultural participation.[13]

In this comparative investigation only one aspect of readership was taken into account — the frequency of reading. However, the investigation of reading frequency also revealed the social range of reading habits and the reading intensity of each social category.

As different investigators use different criteria to measure readership, it is difficult and sometimes impossible to make comparisons not only between countries but also within the same country. As A. Kłoskowska states, 'Polish investigations of readership have been using different criteria based, among other things, on reading frequency. Yet, the reading of books is not a continuous and rhythmical process. Therefore its intensity should rather be measured by the number of books read in a time unit.'[14] Since the beginning of the 1970s, the quantitative criteria used for measuring readership have gradually become more uniform and the criterion proposed by A. Kłoskowska has been used, along with others, in many investigations including that of the Polish Central Statistical Office.[15] A similar criterion was used in the Polish/Hungarian comparative investigation. We assumed that people who do not read a single book in a year can be assessed as being beyond the impact of books. 'Low reading frequency' is characterized by people who read less than 6 books in a year, 'medium reading frequency' is characterized by the reading of 7-24 books a year, and 'high reading frequency' is characterized by the reading of 24 or more books a year. Comparative readership levels are shown in Table 7. The data show the similarity of the basic proportions in both countries, although in Hungary there are fewer people who do not read at all, and in Poland the percentage of people at the low and medium levels of reading frequency is slightly smaller. However, the differences are insignificant. Table 8 concerns the readership of specialist and scientific books. Both in Hungary and Poland there are twice as many people who do not read specialist and scientific books compared with literature in general, and the medium and high-level reading freqencies also show that there are fewer readers of specialist and scientific literature. The readership of specialist and scientific books is therefore of a narrower range than for general literature, and within this group there is a strong prevalence of low reading frequency. However, in Poland this type of readership is even less extensive than in Hungary.

The smaller range of specialist and scientific readership is due to the fact that such books are more difficult in content and demand some knowledge of the subject. Reading specialist and scientific literature is therefore more strongly correlated with the respondents' educational level. In Poland, Pearson's correlation coefficient for the relationship between the respondent's education and the readership of literature is 0.18 (Hungary, 0.21). The correlation between education and the readership of scientific and specialist literature is 0.21 in Poland and 0.24 in Hungary.

TABLE 7
Readership Levels in Poland and Hungary

	Poland	Hungary
	%	%
Non-readers	22.8	17.6
Low-level readers	37.1	37.5
Medium-level readers	26.1	29.3
High-level readers	14.0	15.6

TABLE 8
Readership Levels in Specialist and Scientific Books

	Poland	Hungary
	%	%
Non-readers	45.5	38.1
Low-level readers	38.5	40.5
Medium-level readers	13.8	17.8
High-level readers	2.2	4.4

Such findings are confirmed by the data on readership for the four social categories (Table 9). There is a similar distribution of percentages in the two countries. In both Poland and Hungary there is a clearly marked regularity — the higher the socio-occupational category, the smaller the percentage of people who do not read at all and the greater the percentage of the medium-level and high-level frequency reading. The data show that the distribution of readership is particularly strongly affected by education — reading is lower among manual workers and higher

TABLE 9
Readership of General Literature, According to Socio-occupational Category

Reading frequency levels	Unskilled workers	Skilled workers	White-collar workers	Profes- sionals
	%	%	%	%
Poland				
Total	100.0	100.0	100.0	100.0
Non-readers	32.5	16.9	6.6	4.1
Low-level	38.6	36.3	37.9	30.6
Medium-level	18.4	29.9	38.1	42.5
High-level	10.4	17.5	17.5	22.8
	(*N* = 968)	(*N* = 675)	(*N* = 412)	(*N* = 294)
Hungary				
Total	100.0	100.0	100.0	100.0
Non-readers	28.5	14.2	7.9	2.3
Low-level	36.2	42.6	35.6	27.3
Medium-level	22.4	29.3	38.3	46.8
High-level	13.0	13.9	18.3	23.6
	(*N* = 822)	(*N* = 645)	(*N* = 382)	(*N* = 301)

among non-manual workers. These associations are even higher with regard to specialist and scientific readership (see Table 10).

A detailed analysis of data shows that the reading of literature is more strongly affected by the home than is the reading of scientific and specialist books. Pearson's coefficient shows the correlation between the father's education and reading habits to be 0.17 for Poland and 0.20 for Hungary where literature is concerned, and 0.11 for Poland and 0.15 for Hungary where specialist and scientific books are concerned. If it is assumed that the education of a respondent's father reflects the cultural background of the respondent, some general conclusions can be drawn from the correlation coefficients detected. The readership of specialist and scientific books is more closely correlated with the respondent's occupation, specialization or personal non-occupational interests. On the other hand, the readership of literature is part of a wider pattern of cultural participation, a pattern formed partly by the home. Respondents of families in which the reading of literature was a permanent component exhibit a strong tendency to follow the same pattern, and respondents from families where such reading was only occasional display a lesser tendency to read (Table 11).

TABLE 10

Readership of Specialized and Popular Scientific Literature, According to Socio-occupational Category

Reading frequency levels	**Unskilled workers**	**Skilled workers**	**White-collar workers**	**Profes-sionals**
	%	%	%	%
Poland				
Total	100.0	100.0	100.0	100.0
Non-readers	62.1	32.2	22.1	3.7
Low-level	30.2	47.9	47.3	41.5
Medium-level	6.9	16.9	26.9	42.5
High-level	0.8	3.1	3.6	12.3
	(*N* = 968)	(*N* = 675)	(*N* = 412)	(*N* = 294)
Hungary				
Total	100.0	100.0	100.0	100.0
Non-readers	61.0	26.6	24.1	1.7
Low-level	27.9	54.3	44.0	35.9
Medium-level	8.5	15.9	26.2	46.2
High-level	2.5	3.4	5.7	16.3
	(*N* = 822)	(*N* = 645)	(*N* = 382)	(*N* = 301)

Respondents of the same educational level, but whose fathers have a different level of education, have different attitudes towards the reading of literature. If we take respondents with an elementary education as an example, it can be seen that the reading habit is more strongly developed among respondents whose fathers' education was higher than elementary than among respondents whose fathers also had only an elementary education.

TABLE 11
Respondents Who Have Not Read a Single Book (general literature) in a Year, According to Relationship between Respondents' and Fathers' Education

	Respondent's educational level						
	Elementary		Secondary			University	
	Higher than father's	Same as father's	Higher than father's	Same as father's	Lower than father's	Same as father's	Lower than father's
	%	%	%	%	%	%	%
Poland	14.0	34.1	12.5	16.3	19.5	1.3	7.6
Hungary	17.4	28.0	8.0	9.7	12.0	2.5	4.2

The highest percentage of non-readers is among respondents whose fathers had a lower level of education than their own. The data support the hypothesis that the cultural level of a respondent's home significantly affects the reading habits of the respondent.[16] There is a two-generational influence at work — reading habits are strengthened by a consistently high cultural level and lessened by a low cultural level. The least favourable syndrome of factors in both countries is when both father and respondent have only an elementary level of education. This group contains the highest percentage of non-readers — Poland 34.1 percent and Hungary 28 percent. The most favourable syndrome exists when both father and respondent have had a university education. The percentage of non-readers is the lowest in this group — Poland 1.3 percent and Hungary 2.5 percent.

As reading habits are similar in Hungary and Poland, it is possible to conclude that the process of transmitting reading habits is relatively universal in character.

Model 3: Cultural Activities Outside the Home

Our data confirm the thesis that particular forms of cultural activity differ in social range. Some kinds reach all social categories (i.e. television) and others reach only a part, and sometimes a very small part, of the population. Table 12 illustrates the number of people who do not participate in various forms of cultural activity, i.e., people beyond the range of the specified cultural institutions. Figure 1, based on the data, graphically illustrates the social range of cultural institutions in Poland and Hungary.

TABLE 12
Percentage not Participating in Various Cultural Activities

	Poland	Hungary
	%	%
Cinema	34	32
Sports matches	53	50
Pop music concerts	55	79
Circuses	59	59
Museums	61	36
Exhibitions	63	39
Theatre	63	48
Operettas	76	83
Opera	88	91
Classical music concerts	91	87

Music (opera, operetta, classical music) has the smallest audience. This part of the population is sometimes defined by sociologists as the 'cultural elite'. On the other hand, only a third of the population in both countries do not go to the cinema.

Although the patterns are broadly similar in Poland and Hungary, the investigation reveals certain significant differences in specific features of cultural participation in the two countries. In Hungary there is a distinctly higher percentage of people who do not attend pop music concerts, while in Poland there are more people who do not frequent museums, exhibitions and the theatre.

If the coefficients of correlation between the different kinds of cultural activity are analysed, certain forms are more highly correlated with each other than are others. There is a positive correlation between going to museums and exhibitions (Poland 0.45 and Hungary 0.55). In Hungary there is a significant correlation between going to classical music concerts and the opera ($r = 0.36$); in Poland this coefficient is much lower ($r = 0.19$).

In both countries the investigation shows a significant correlation between going to the theatre and symphony concerts, the theatre and opera, the theatre and museums, and the theatre and exhibitions. There are also significant correlations between going to the theatre and operettas.

The reading of literature gains in intensity, particularly in Hungary, with the growth of participation in other cultural activities. The data show, however, that the majority of cultural activities under discussion are connected with a small group of people. The question then arises of whether these cultural activities that enjoy so little popularity are determined by socio-occupational category, i.e. express a specific cultural participation pattern of certain categories, or whether they are a marginal activity for all social groups. Such a question is directly connected with the issue of whether or not manual and non-manual workers have been brought closer together. A synthetic index was worked out to distinguish two groups of people from the cultural advancement point of view — the group classified as recipients of culture transmitted by certain cultural institutions, and the group beyond the range of these cultural institutions.

The first group — the active recipients of culture — included respondents who read 13 or more books a year, and who participate twice or more in at least three of the following activities: theatre, classical music concerts, opera, museums and exhibitions.

The second group — the passive recipients of culture — included respondents who do not read a single book a year, and do not participate in the other activities listed above. These two groups represent the extremes in terms of institutionalized cultural participation, as the first group, which not only engages in relaxing

FIGURE 1
People who Do Not Participate in the Following Forms of Cultural Activity

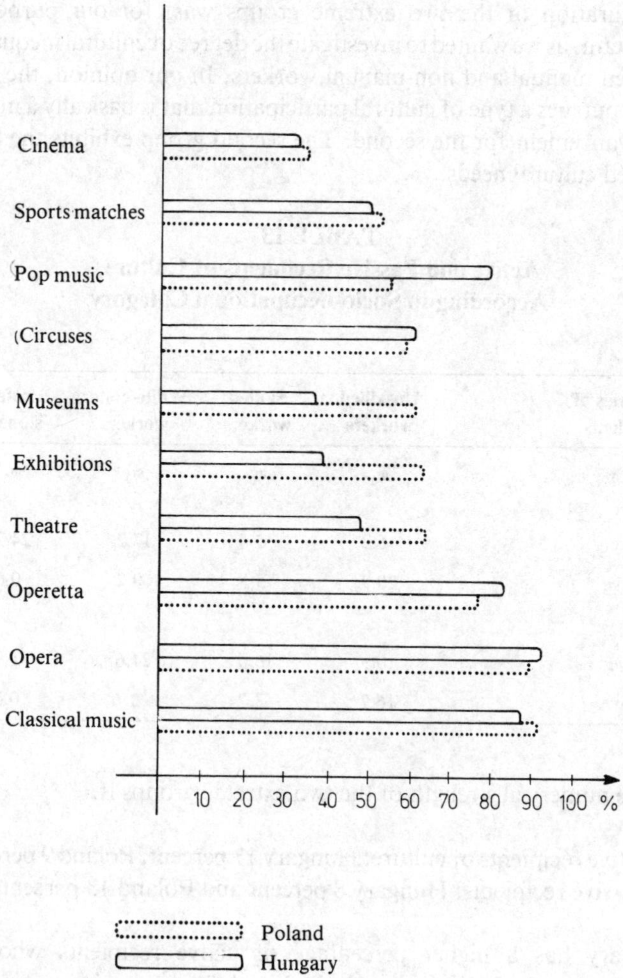

and entertaining cultural activities but also seeks intellectual and aesthetic experiences, is in direct contrast to the second group. There is an intermediate group between the two extremes, which only occasionally participates in such cultural activities, which thus are not a permanent component of their culture.

An investigation of the numerical strength and the social configuration of the two extreme groups was, for our purposes, important, as we wanted to investigate the degree of cultural inequality between manual and non-manual workers. In our opinion, the first group pursues a type of cultural participation that is basically a model of advancement for the second. The second group exhibits the least aroused cultural needs.

TABLE 13
Active and Passive Recipients of Culture, According to Socio-occupational Category

Categories of respondents	Unskilled workers	Skilled workers	White-collar workers	Profes-sionals
	%	%	%	%
Poland				
Active	5.2	8.6	17.2	24.2
Passive	20.9	5.5	0.2	0.0
Hungary				
Active	10.9	16.0	24.6	41.9
Passive	16.7	3.7	1.6	0.0

The numerical strength of the two extreme groups is:

(1) active recipients of culture: Hungary 17 percent, Poland 9 percent;
(2) passive recipients: Hungary 8 percent and Poland 13 percent.

Hungary has a higher percentage of active recipients who are sometimes called the 'cultural elite' and fewer passive recipients, people sometimes called the culturally backward (see Table 13). In both countries there is the same regularity — the higher the socio-occupational category, the larger the number of active recipients of culture. In Hungary the percentage of active recipients in all the social categories is twice as high as in Poland. The passive recipients are represented mainly by unskilled workers (Poland 21 percent and Hungary 17 percent); there are no professionals in this group.

TABLE 14
Active and Passive Recipients, According to Relationship between Respondent's and Father's Education

	Poland			Hungary		
	Father's education in relation to that of respondent					
	Higher	Same	Lower	Higher	Same	Lower
	%	%	%	%	%	%
Respondents with elementary education						
Active	14.7	3.9	—	15.1	8.0	—
Passive	6.2	22.3	—	7.0	16.5	—
Respondents with secondary education						
Active	18.8	13.0	9.6	36.0	29.0	16.7
Passive	0.0	3.3	7.8	0.0	1.2	4.3
Respondents with university education						
Active	—	29.5	13.7	—	45.0	35.0
Passive	—	0.0	0.6	—	0.0	0.0

The data show that both in Hungary and Poland social differentiation in terms of participation in cultural activities is clearly marked. Such differentiation is due not only to different educational levels in each social category, but also to different cultural levels at home (see Table 14). Furthermore, respondents' education alone does not fully explain the differences in levels of cultural activity. When a respondent's father has a higher level of education than the respondent, the respondent himself is more apt to be an active recipient. Among respondents with a university education whose fathers also had a university education, more respondents were active recipients of culture than respondents whose fathers had a level of education lower than their own. The impact of the home is even more clearly marked when respondents had an elementary or secondary education.

The data confirm, to a certain extent, R. Boudon's thesis that the higher the educational level, the lesser the impact of the home.[17] However, this impact never completely disappears.

The more general conclusion, that cultural inequalities are not due solely to a respondent's current social position, can be drawn from the results of our analysis. The sources of such inequalities go deeper and are to be found in the cultural level of the home, which shapes cultural participation habits during the early stages of the socialization process.

CULTURAL ASPIRATIONS

Cultural aspirations were investigated to see if respondents' aspirations were similar to their actual cultural participation. The respondents were asked the question: 'Would you like to spend more of your spare time on the following activities (14 activities enumerated)?' There were four possible answers: (1) as much time as now, (2) a little more time than now, (3) more time than now, (4) much more time than now. Table 15 shows the correlation between the pursuit of a given type of cultural activity and the respondent's willingness to spend more time on it.

The investigation shows a relatively strong positive correlation between the actual frequency of pursuing a given activity and the willingness to spend more time on it. The more often people pursue a given activity, the more time they would like to have for it. However, this statement does not apply to all cultural activities, as the frequency of watching television and willingness to spend more time on it is not correlated at all.

In Poland there is no correlation between going to the cinema and the willingness to spend more time doing so, but in Hungary there is a positive correlation. There is a clearly marked correlation with regard to the theatre, classical music concerts (particularly in Hungary), opera, operetta and exhibitions, and the strongest correlation exists as far as sports matches and pop concerts are concerned.

TABLE 15
Coefficients of Correlation between Actual and Desired Frequency of Pursuing Selected Cultural Activities

Activities	Poland	Hungary
Literature	0.09	0.19
Specialized and popular scientific books	0.14	0.20
Cinema	0.02	0.13
Television	−0.08	−0.02
Theatre	0.23	0.26
Classical music concerts	0.22	0.40
Opera	0.23	0.29
Operetta	0.29	0.25
Exhibitions	0.26	0.28
Pop music concerts	0.32	0.41
Sports matches	0.49	0.40

The basis on which answers were graded meant that a mean number of points could be calculated for each activity. The mean value shows the general direction of differentiation according to social category. However, as with every mean value, it obliterates actual differences within the population and shows only general tendencies. The data in Table 16 show the mean number of points per activity.

These data point to quite significant differences between representatives of each social category. The higher the social category, the higher the average aspirations in the sphere of such cultural activities as the reading of literature and specialized books, and visits to the theatre and classical music concerts. At the same time, a higher socio-occupational status indicates lower aspirations in relation to such activities as television-viewing and visits to a circus or sports match. Only cinema-going is a typical inter-category activity — an activity that does not seem to depend on a respondent's social position. Considering the fact that the general tendencies are analogous, it can be suggested that there is a relatively permanent and universalistic divergence of orientations towards individual kinds of activities. If this hypothesis could be confirmed by further investigations, the question of cultural advancement would then be regarded slightly differently. Different aspirations in each social category would mean that the cultural pattern followed by the professionals does not have to be the cultural advancement model for all representatives of the other social categories.

TABLE 16
Mean Number of Points for Aspirations as Related to Chosen Activities, According to Socio-occupational Categories

Chosen cultural activities	Unskilled workers	Skilled workers	White-collar workers	Profes-sionals
Poland				
Literature	2.0	2.2	2.5	2.7
Specialized books	1.6	2.0	2.2	2.5
Cinema	1.9	2.1	2.1	2.1
Television	1.8	1.6	1.5	1.2
Theatre	1.9	2.1	2.4	2.7
Classical music concerts	1.2	1.3	1.5	1.7
Circuses	1.9	1.7	1.4	1.2
Sports matches	1.9	2.0	1.7	1.6
Hungary				
Literature	2.2	2.3	2.5	2.7
Specialized books	1.7	2.1	2.2	2.5
Cinema	1.9	2.1	2.0	1.9
Television	2.0	1.9	1.6	1.3
Theatre	2.0	2.3	2.6	2.6
Classical music concerts	1.3	1.4	1.7	1.9
Circuses	1.9	1.7	1.4	1.2
Sports matches	2.0	2.0	1.9	1.6

Pearson's correlation coefficients show that professional people, while pursuing their favourite cultural activities, show quite strong aspirations to increase the frequency of such activities. However, in some activities the aspirations of professionals are lower than the aspirations of manual workers (and of unskilled workers in particular).

Such results favour the hypothesis that there are certain specific cultural participation patterns (institutionalized forms of cultural transmission) that are not only followed, but also desired by members of each social category.

TABLE 17
Respondents Who Would Like to Spend More Time* on Chosen Cultural Activity, According to Relationship between Respondent's and Father's Levels of Education

	Respondent's educational level *						
	Elementary		Secondary			University	
Chosen cultural activities	Higher than father's	Same as father's	Higher than father's	Same as father's	Lower than father's	Same as father's	Lower than father's
	%	%	%	%	%	%	%
Poland							
Literature	63.6	61.4	71.9	52.7	67.0	71.8	76.4
Television	44.2	49.8	37.5	27.5	47.3	26.9	29.7
Theatre	65.9	52.4	71.9	63.7	66.3	88.9	77.8
Classical music	21.7	12.5	40.6	19.8	16.0	33.0	27.3
Hungary							
Literature	73.3	67.6	76.0	77.5	75.6	87.5	81.7
Television	48.8	60.2	40.0	42.8	52.5	75.0	30.0
Theatre	65.1	60.0	68.0	76.9	77.0	82.5	83.3
Classical music	29.1	19.3	50.0	41.4	31.5	55.0	56.3

*'More' answers: 'a little more', 'more' and 'much more'.
Elementary: 8 years or less
Secondary: 9-12 years
University: more than 12 years.

There are certain general tendencies that do not show any

significant social differentiation, but the data in Table 17 only reveal the part played by the home in shaping cultural aspirations. For the purpose of our survey, respondents with elementary education were divided into two groups: (1) respondents whose fathers' educational level is higher than elementary and (2) respondents whose educational level is the same as their fathers'.The difference in the cultural aspirations of these two groups is due to the impact of the home. Table 17 shows the impact to be quite clearly marked with respect to television, theatre and classical music concerts among respondents with an elementary education. There are similar tendencies in both countries, although the extent of differences varies. In Poland the percentage of people who would like to spend more time watching television is 44 percent in the first group and 50 percent in the second group (Hungary 49 and 60 percent). In both countries, when the level of education of the respondent's father is higher then elementary, television aspirations are lower. However, the education of the father has a stronger effect in Hungary than in Poland.

There is a different situation with regard to aspirations concerning the theatre. The percentage of people willing to spend more time on this activity in the first group is 66 percent for Poland and 65 percent for Hungary, and the percentage in the second group is 52 percent for Poland and 60 percent for Hungary. In both countries aspirations regarding theatre attendance are strengthened when the repondents' father has a higher level of education then elementary.

The father's educational level has a similar effect on respondent's aspirations concerning classical music concerts. When the father's education exceeds that of a respondent, the respondent is more willing to spend more time on that cultural activity.

Although the educational level of a respondent's father has an effect on respondents with a secondary or university education, the higher the education, the smaller is the difference in aspirations.

It is thus possible to conclude that respondents with the same formal education show different cultural aspirations because they are to a large extent shaped by the cultural level of the home.

The view that the cultural level of the home is essentially correlated with a respondent's cultural participation pattern can be extended, as the home affects not only the actual cultural behaviour but also cultural aspirations.

In our opinion, the investigation proves that both in Hungary and Poland there is what can be called a relatively permanent, inter-generationally reproduced cultural participation pattern, and such a pattern includes cultural aspirations.

Social mobility processes, particularly in the sphere of education, are connected with cultural mobility processes but do not produce automatic changes. Where there is inter-generational 'degradation in education', the impact of home weakens the analogical 'degradation' in the sphere of cultural activities and cultural aspirations. On the other hand, where there is inter-generational advancement in educational terms, the impact of home weakens the analogical 'advancement' in the sphere of cultural activities and aspirations.

LEAVE FROM WORK

Our survey covered three questions in relation to paid time off. The investigation dealt with differences, or their lack, in amount of formal time off work among manual and non-manual workers, the utilization of spare time, and the extent to which the basic function of spare time — rest — was met in the different social categories.

An attempt was made at defining time off in the two countries but the data ultimately presented in Table 18 are based on respondents' declarations and these were not verified. Although this comparative research covered several aspects regarding time off, only those issues were selected that, in our opinion, were of fundamental importance for the explanation of certain social inequalities. We regarded a day as reserved for rest if the respondent utilized the time for recreation, that is he/she did not do domestic work or work outside for a wage.

TABLE 18
Average Yearly Leave (in days)

	Hungary	Poland
Statutory	18.9	23.2
Utilized	18.1	21.4
Reserved for rest	10.6	16.8

In Poland there is more time off than in Hungary, and as a result more holiday days are taken and more days are reserved for rest. If, however, we inspect the precentages, it turns out that a longer statutory time off work does not mean a proportional growth in its utilization, or a larger number of days reserved for relaxation. In Hungary time off is more fully utilized, and in Poland more time is spent 'resting'. In Poland 78 percent and in Hungary 60 percent of utilized time off is reserved for 'rest' (Table 19).

TABLE 19
Average Time Off Work, According to Socio-occupational Categories

	Average time off work (days per year)			
	Unskilled workers	**Skilled workers**	**White-collar workers**	**Profes-sionals**
Poland				
Statutory	22.5	22.6	24.1	24.0
Utilized	21.9	21.6	21.1	19.4
Reserved for rest	16.9	16.6	17.6	16.1
Hungary				
Statutory	18.5	18.7	20.0	19.4
Utilized	17.9	18.1	19.0	17.6
Reserved for rest	8.8	9.9	12.4	13.7

In both Poland and Hungary, professionals and white-collar workers have more leave than manual workers (1.5-0.7 more days), but with regard to time off actually utilized the situation is a little different. In both countries, leave is least utilized by professional people. However, the data show that the number of days reserved by each social category for 'rest' is much more differentiated in Hungary than in Poland. In Poland only white-collar workers differed in this respect from the other social categories, but in Hungary an increase in the number of days reserved for 'rest' accompanies a rise in the socio-occupational categories (from 8.8 days among unskilled workers to 13.7 days among professionals).

Table 20 shows what part of the utilized time off is reserved for rest by each social category. The data show that in Hungary the proportion of leave that is taken and devoted to relaxation increases with each rise in socio-occupational status, from 50 percent in the first category to over 80 percent in the fourth category. In Poland there is not so great a differentiation in this respect, but white-collar workers and professionals do reserve a larger part of their time off for rest than do manual workers.

TABLE 20
Percentage of Number of Days Off

	Hungary	Poland
Unskilled workers	50	77
Skilled workers	59	77
White-collar workers	64	83
Professionals	81	83

Our analysis of the utilization of leave in both countries is based on the average number of days taken, but behind that average number there are significant forms of differentiation that affect the overall distribution of data. In Poland the percentage of people who do not reserve a single day of their utilized leave for rest is similar in all social categories. In Hungary this percentage is higher in the first three social categories, and there is a decreasing tendency as the categories rise (from 33 percent in the first category to 8 percent in the fourth category).

TABLE 21
Percentage of Respondents Who Did Not Go on Holiday

	Hungary	Poland
Unskilled workers	17	42
Skilled workers	9	32
White-collar workers	9	21
Professionals	4	18

The data show that Hungarian industrial workers are more

inclined to reserve their time off for purposes other than rest, than are the Poles. However, it is not unlikely that the empirical data have assumed these values owing to a different understanding of 'rest' in the two countries. We suspect that Hungarian respondents understood the notion of rest somewhat differently, and did not include activities that Polish respondents regarded as part of rest. The data of Table 21 should, therefore, be treated with reserve.

It can be seen from the table that, as the socio-occupational status rises, the number of people who do not go away on holiday becomes relatively smaller, but there is much less difference in Hungary than in Poland: 10.6 percent of respondents in Poland, and 24.2 percent of respondents in Hungary, declared that they spent at least part of their holidays abroad. In Hungary greater territorial mobility correlates with a larger number of people going abroad, while in Poland, where there is less territorial mobility, a lower proportion of people go abroad. Holidays spent abroad differ according to social category (Table 22). The higher the socio-occupational category, the higher the percentage of people spending at least part of their free time abroad. The data again prove that there is an essential difference in the pattern of use of free time between manual and non-manual workers, particularly if the two extreme categories are compared.

TABLE 22
Percentage of Respondents Spending Holidays Abroad

	Hungary	Poland
Unskilled workers	10	6
Skilled workers	20	8
White-collar workers	25	17
Professionals	34	23

In spite of the fact that in Poland there is more time off and more time spent on rest, the rate of days spent abroad as related to the average number of days used for rest is much larger in Hungary than in Poland. In Hungary an average of 17 percent of free days is spent abroad, while in Poland the average is 7.7 percent. This indicator is clearly differentiated according to socio-occupational category (Table 23). Going abroad is rather a marginal part of the pattern of using free time among unskilled workers, while it is an important part of the pattern among professionals. In Poland 20 percent of the days used for rest among professionals is used for foreign travel, while in Hungary the figure is 28 percent.

TABLE 23
Percentage of Days Off Spent Abroad, by Socio-occupational Category

	Hungary	Poland
Unskilled workers	10	4
Skilled workers	19	6
White-collar workers	19	12
Professionals	28	20

Generally speaking, the distribution of the empirical data shows that in Hungary people do go away from home during their holidays, although a significant section of such people do not regard such an activity as 'rest'. In Poland, according to respondents' declarations, most free time is connected with some kind of leisure activity. However, there is less territorial mobility in Poland than in Hungary.

A more detailed analysis, which would take into account the social context of both countries, is required. Although it is not unlikely that respondents in Hungary and Poland have a different idea of holiday 'rest', there are certain additional variables that have some impact. Table 24, citing holiday preferences, is indicative of these.

The data in the table point to certain characteristic tendencies. In Hungary both manual and non-manual workers show a clearly marked tendency for free time to be spent in holiday accommodation in their own country. In Poland the attractiveness of such holidays decreases with the rise in socio-occupational status (51 percent in the first category, 20 percent in the fourth). In both countries the attractiveness of individual tourism grows with the rise in socio-occupational status. In Hungary this tendency applies to tourism abroad (17 percent in the first category, 45 percent in the fourth), and in Poland it applies to tourism at home (13 percent in the first category, 46 percent in the fourth). It is probable that in Hungary there is a stronger orientation towards trips abroad. The attractiveness of holidays in tourist accommodation abroad is similar in both countries, and does not show any important differentiation according to social category. Holidays spent at home grow less attractive with the rise in socio-occupational status This kind of holiday is more valued in Hungary (41 percent in the first category, 9 percent in the fourth) than in Poland (20 percent in the first category, 3 percent in the fourth). This differentiation is probably connected with the fact that in Poland more respondents do spend their holidays inside the country and therefore find such a kind of holiday less attractive than do respondents in Hungary. In both countries certain types of holiday are seen by respondents as particularly attractive — tourism at home, rented rooms in summer resorts (particularly in Hungary) and a stay with relatives (particularly in Poland).

TABLE 24
Holiday Preferences, According to Socio-occupational Categories

	Unskilled workers		Skilled workers		White-collar workers		Professionals	
	Poland (*N*=965)	Hungary (*N*=810)	Poland (*N*=674)	Hungary (*N*=639)	Poland (*N*=411)	Hungary (*N*=376)	Poland (*N*=294)	Hungary (*N*=296)
	%	%	%	%	%	%	%	%
In holiday house in own country	51.3	50.0	42.4	46.6	36.2	55.0	20.1	40.9
In holiday house abroad	21.4	19.0	21.8	20.0	25.8	21.8	18.4	22.3
Individual tourism abroad	12.7	17.5	23.6	30.0	24.1	28.5	39.5	45.3
Organized tours abroad	17.9	17.3	18.8	18.9	28.7	27.1	26.9	26.7
Individual tourism in own country	12.7	12.0	25.4	18.8	28.7	15.2	46.3	24.0
In own holiday cottage	19.1	9.6	19.6	14.2	19.2	12.8	19.0	16.5
Visiting relatives	13.8	18.0	9.5	12.4	4.1	6.4	2.0	6.8
Organized tours in own country	8.8	7.5	12.6	6.1	13.4	9.3	8.8	2.7
In rented room in summer resort	10.2	2.1	6.4	2.2	5.3	1.9	7.1	1.7
At home	20.1	41.4	10.4	25.5	5.1	19.1	2.7	9.5

CONCLUSION

Although our investigation was limited to a primary quantitative approach, dealing only with that proportion of the urban population employed in industry and their participation in institutionalized forms of culture, the results of the investigation support our hypothesis concerning the pattern of reproduction of cultural participation and the changing role of the media in cultural transmission in the social context. The main conclusions to be drawn from the comparative data are as follows.

1. In Poland and in Hungary television-viewing is part of the daily routine of the majority of industrial workers, but television is less attractive to professional people than any other social category. For professionals television is but one of the components of a richer and more diversified pattern of cultural activity, but where the other social categories are concerned it frequently substitutes for other kinds of cultural activity. In both countries there is a certain sub-population for which television is the only medium of cultural transmission. This sub-population consists of people with a low level of education, in an older age group, and from a low social status background.

2. In comparison to general readership levels, the readership of specialized and scientific books is smaller in its social range and is more closely correlated with the respondent's occupation, specialization or individual non-occupational interests. The readership of general literature is a part of a wider pattern of cultural participation — a pattern partly formed by the home. It can be assumed that respondents from families in which the reading of books was habitual show a stronger tendency to follow the same pattern of behaviour than do respondents from families where such reading was only occasional. The data show that, in both countries, respondents on the same educational level, but with fathers with a different level of education, show different attitudes towards reading; for example, among respondents with an elementary level of education there is a clearly marked difference between respondents whose fathers had an elementary education and respondents whose fathers had a higher-than-elementary education. There is a higher percentage of people who do not read at all when the father's education is lower than that of the respondent. Data, therefore, confirm the hypothesis that the cultural level of a respondent's home significantly affects his/her reading habits. There is a two-generational transmission of reading habits — a high cultural level at home strengthens, and a low cultural level at home lessens, contact with literature. As the data for Hungary and

Poland were similar in this respect, it can be concluded that the process of transmitting reading habits is relatively universal in character, as is the case with other forms of cultural activities.

3. Data on cultural activities support a more general thesis that cultural inequalities in both countries are due not only to the respondents' social position. The sources of such inequalities are to be found in the cultural level of the home, which shapes cultural habits during early stages of the socialization process: for example, those among the professional category who are the first generation to possess a degree reveal their earlier cultural participation patterns.

4. The data on cultural aspirations point to quite significant differences between the socio-occupational categories. The higher the respondents' socio-occupational status, the higher the average aspirations in the sphere of such cultural activities as reading (of both general literature and specialized books), and going to the theatre or classical music concerts. Such respondents also have lower aspirations with regard to the watching of television or going to a circus or sports match. Only cinema-going is an inter-category activity. The fact that there are similar general tendencies in both countries allows us to surmise that there is a relatively permanent and more universal divergence of orientations towards individual activities, and the question of cultural advancement should thus be regarded in a slightly different context. Different aspirations in different social categories mean that the cultural patterns followed by the professionals do not necessarily have to represent the model of cultural advancement for the other social categories.

5. The comparative investigation demonstrates that in Poland and Hungary there are processes that can be viewed as a relatively permanent, inter-generationally reproduced, cultural participation pattern which is also the key to cultural aspirations. Social mobility processes, particularly in the field of education, are connected with cultural mobility processes but do not produce automatic changes. Where there is inter-generational 'degradation' through education, the impact of the home weakens any analogical 'degradation' in the sphere of cultural activity and cultural aspirations. On the other hand, given inter-generational advancement through education, the impact of the home weakens the analogical cultural advancement.

The investigation of the use of free time shows that industrial workers have more leave from work in Poland than they do in Hungary. However, the differences between manual and non-manual workers are similar, with both Hungarian and Polish professionals and white-collar workers having longer holidays than manual workers.

In Poland respondents spend more time at 'rest' than in Hungary, but in Hungary more people spend more of their holidays at home. In both countries a rise in socio-occupational status results in a relatively smaller number of people who do not go away on holidays. In Hungary, because territorial mobility is greater than in Poland, a substantially larger proportion of people spend their holidays abroad. Trips abroad are correlated with socio-occupational status — the higher the status, the higher the percentage taking trips abroad.

Generally speaking, the investigation supports the thesis that there are substantial inequalities among industrial workers, and particularly between manual and non-manual workers. The inequalities appeared (1) in the sphere of formal time off work, (2) in the length of leave actually utilized, (3) in the length of time devoted to the basic function of leave from work — 'rest'. In these three dimensions non-manual workers are in a better position than manual workers. From the social point of view, this problem deserves further investigation.

NOTES

1. See A. Kłoskowska, *Społeczne ramy kultury*, (Social Framework of Culture), Warsaw, 1972; Z. Bokszański, *Młodzi robotnicy i awans kulturalny*, (Young Workers and Cultural Advancement), Warsaw, 1976.

2. See A. Tyszka, *Uczestnictwo w kulturze*, (Cultural Participation), Warsaw, 1971; M. Czerwiński, *Kultura i jej badanie*, (Culture and Research), Wrocław, 1971.

3. K. Zagórski, 'Zagadnienia badawcze struktury i ruchliwości społecznej klasy robotniczej' ('Research on the Structure and Social Mobility of the Working Class'), in *Teoretyczne i metodologiczne problemy statystyki społecznej* (Theoretical and methodological problems of social statistics), Warsaw, 1970.

4. K. Słomczyński, *Zróznicowanie społeczno-zawodowe i jego korelaty* (Socio-occupational Differentiation and its Correlates), Wrocław, 1972, p. 13.

5. P. Bourdieu, 'Reproduction culturelle et reproduction sociale', *Information sur les Sciences Sociales*, vol. X, no. 2, 1971, pp. 45-79; Bokszański, op. cit., pp. 44-5.

6. R. Dyoniziak, *Zróżnicowanie kulturowe społeczności wielkomiejskiej*, (Cultural Differentiation of Large Urban Communities), Warsaw, 1969.

7. Bokszański, op. cit., p. 259.

8. My own calculations of the basis of *Budżet czasu rodzin pracowniczych*(Time Budget in Working Families), GUS (Central Statistical Office), Warsaw, 1970, and L.Adamczuk;Budżet czasu mieszkańców Polski (Time Budget of Polish Inhabitants) Warsaw, 1969.

9. G. Fukasz, 'Saturday Off and Weekend and Leisure Habits of Hungarian Workers', in *Leisure and Education*, Budapest, 1974.

10. Elementary — 8 years or fewer (for Poland N = 869, for Hungary N = 672); secondary — 9-12 years (for Poland N = 406, for Hungary N = 981); university — more than 12 years (for Poland N = 420, for Hungary N = 160).

11. R. Boudon, *Education, Opportunity and Social Inequality*, New York, London, Sydney and Toronto, 1974.

12. E.E. Wnuk-Lipiński; *Problematyka kształtowania sie potrzeb czytelniczych* (Formation of Reading Needs), Warsaw, 1975, p. 23.

13. J. Ankudowicz, *Czytelnictwo na tle życia kulturalnego i struktury społecznej mieszkańców małych miast* (Readership against the Background of Cultural Life and Social Structure of Small Towns), Warsaw, 1967; A. Pawełczyńska, *Studia nad czytelnictwem* (Studies of Readership), Warsaw, 1969.

14. B. Barelson; 'Who Reads What Books and Why', in B. Rosenberg and D.M. White (eds), *Mass Culture,* 1957.

15. A. Kłoskowska; *Społeczne ramy kultury* (Social Framework of Culture), Warsaw, 1972, p. 156.

16. Wnuk-Lipiński, op. cit.

17. Boudon, op. cit., p. 86.

CONCLUDING REMARKS: Inconsistencies and Inequalities

Tamás Kolosi

At the end of our analysis, the connection between, and the joint effect of, the separate elements investigated (work, material living conditions and mobility) on the stratification of industrial workers has to be examined. The most satisfactory explanation of the differences between workers is obtained by dividing them into socio-occupational groups.[1] It can be concluded that this form of stratification is most closely connected with work, while cultural activities, material living conditions and mobility sometimes consolidate this hierarchy but also can cut across it and cause considerable status inconsistencies.[2]

In our analysis we applied multivariate mathematical methods and selected a few variables in each domain for this purpose, namely those that could be subject to ordinal scaling (which is a precondition for the use of such methods).

In the field of *work* and *working conditions*, the manual and intellectual demands of various occupations, the qualifications necessary for a given job, working hours and an aggregate index of the social activity[3] were taken into account. Where *material living conditions* were concerned, the absolute incomes, the per capita income of the family and a combined index representing possession of consumer durable goods were used. In the field of *cultural activities*, in addition to the number of days spent on recreation and holidays, as well as reading frequency, two special variables were created: the degree of participation in so-called 'high culture' (theatre, opera, concerts and exhibitions) and the extent of participation in popular forms of cultural entertainment (cinema, operetta, circus and light music). In operationalizing *mobility,* the educational level of the father, the mother and the spouse were employed. Although earlier analyses have indicated that, where parents and spouse are concerned, their socio-occupational group is more important as a determinant, mainly because of the different character of agriculture in the two countries together with their historical differences, nevertheless, as we could not elaborate an ordinal ranking of socio-occupational groups, we adhered to the educational level instead.

In addition to these four dimensions, we also took into consideration a few other variables, which characterized the *socio-demographic* situation of the respondents, as we considered such factors to be of importance from the point of view of stratification. Among these variables was the socio-occupational group, created from the basic variables in our investigation in the following manner:

1. unskilled workers (unskilled workers and semi-skilled workers without a dominant task);
2. unskilled foremen;
3. skilled workers (without dominant task);
4. administrative-clerical workers (clerks without higher education);
5. skilled foremen;
6. medium-level managers (white-collar but without higher education);
7. professionals (with higher education);
8. managers (department heads or top intellectuals).

In addition to educational level, the respondent's age, character of housing and (as the strongest differentiating variable within families) number of children in his/her household were taken into consideration.

The first step in the analysis was the canonic correlation[4] of these five dimensions (see Table 1). In both countries the correlation coefficient between the demographic situation and work is the highest of all, but in Hungary it is considerably higher than Poland. In Hungary the connection between these two dimensions is determined by the socio-occupational group and the qualifications necessary to it, while in Poland it is affected by educational level, necessary qualifications and the weight of manual work. The eight-category socio-occupational grouping is therefore better for portraying the internal stratification of industrial workers in Hungary than in Poland, but there is a closer connection between educational level and working conditions in Poland.

TABLE 1
Canonic Correlation Coefficients

	Hungary					Poland				
	1	**2**	**3**	**4**	**5**	**1**	**2**	**3**	**4**	**5**
1. Socio-demographic situation	—	0.81	0.45	0.53	0.58	0.67	0.67	0.61	0.51	0.55
2. Work	—	—	0.40	0.51	0.19	—	—	0.49	0.49	0.20
3. Material living conditions	—	—	—	0.39	0.13	—	—	—	0.44	0.25
4. Culture	—	—	—	—	0.35	—	—	—	—	0.32
5. Mobility	—	—	—	—	—	—	—	—	—	—

The connection between material living conditions and other dimensions is stronger in Poland than in Hungary. This indicates that the 'divergent' differentiation of material living conditions in Hungary causes considerable status inconsistencies, while in Poland the transmission of material living conditions, according to background, and the present social situation are more congruent. In both countries the relationship between work, culture and material living conditions is stronger than any connection with mobility. This points to the fact that the existing differences are greater than the extent to which these differences are reproduced.

If the variables that primarily determine the canonic correlations are examined, then the differences between the two countries are not very significant. For example, from among variables indicative of the socio-demographic situation, the socio-occupational group has a greater effect in Hungary, while in Poland the effect of the educational level is stronger.[5] In Hungary the influence of social background is determined almost exclusively by the situation of the father, while in Poland the effect of the mother's situation is greater. Finally, holidays in Hungary are differentiated more by socio-demographic factors and material living conditions than is the case in Poland.

In both countries there is a close connection between age and material living conditions, or between age and participation in popular culture, between working conditions and income or consumption, between background and housing, and between cultural activities and the spouse's educational level or type of social activity. If the aggregate variance of all the variables examined is calculated for both countries, one component alone explains around 50 percent of the total variance.[6] In both countries this component is closely connected with socio-occupational group, the qualifications necessary for it, educational level, the intellectual demands of work and participation in 'high culture' — only this relative contribution differs. There is a bigger cross-national difference when weak connections with this chief component are examined (those under 0.2). In Hungary the educational level of the mother, the income of the family, the age and the number of children, and in Poland the income of the family, are weakly connected with it. These factors thus largely cut across the stratificational hierarchy (see Table 2).

Pursuing our analysis of the chief component, we carried out a factor analysis using the SPSS Varimax rotation.[7] In both countries six factors were obtained. The first factor dominant in Hungary was the socio-occupational group and those variables connected with work, while in Poland the dominant factor was the variables connected with work, with the educational-occupational variables occupying a secondary position. In Poland educational level, socio-educational group and the manual demands of work represented the fourth factor, while in Hungary the manual demands of work, working hours, housing situation and the character of housing were separate. This indicates that in Poland there is a fundamentally greater inconsistency between actual work and the social-educational-occupational groups than in Hungary. In Hungary the cluster of workers in heavy manual jobs, with several shifts and thus unfavourable work schedules, and a high proportion of workers living in villages, form a separate and distinctive group within the occupational structure. The unfavourable housing conditions of this group largely account for the differentiation in housing situation among the total population.

The second factor in both countries includes the educational level of the parents, but it is only very weakly connected with other variables. This shows that background, which is substantially independent from the other variables examined, nevertheless exerts a relatively strong influence on differentiating between industrial workers.

TABLE 2
The Connection between the Mean Component and the Variables

	Hungary		Poland	
	r	Order	*r*	Order
Socio-occupational group	0.82	1	0.70	3
Necessary qualification	0.79	2	0.71	2
Education level	0.78	3	0.82	1
Intellectual weighting of work	0.69	4	0.62	4
High culture	0.64	5	0.62	5
Reading	0.55	6	0.56	6
Social activity	0.51	7	0.42	10
Manual weight of work	−0.47	8	−0.47	8
Consumer durable goods	0.44	9	0.50	7
Holidays	0.35	10	0.25	14
Work schedule	0.32	11	0.23	17
Housing location	0.29	12	0.20	20
Mother's educational level	0.29	13	0.35	11
Entertainment	0.24	14	0.43	9
Housing situation	0.22	15	0.27	13
Income	0.21	16	0.35	12
Father's educational level	0.20	17	0.25	15
Spouse's educational level	0.16	18	0.25	16
Income per capita	0.10	19	0.06	21
Age	−0.09	20	−0.22	18
Number of children	0.08	21	0.21	19

Rank correlation coefficient = 0.87

The third factor in Hungary is dominated by demographic features (spouse, age, number of children), together with participation in popular cultural activity, although the latter is of secondary importance. In Poland relative importance is reversed and this factor — i.e., participation in entertainment and 'high culture' together with frequency of reading — has primacy, while age and spouse's educational level appear as secondary factors.

In Hungary the fifth factor is made up of variables relative to cultural activity and holidays as well as the supply of consumer durable goods. In Poland the fifth factor concerns various aspects of material living conditions. The housing situation, supply of consumer durable goods, place of residence and holidays (because of its connection with place of residence) cluster together. Of secondary importance is age and participation in 'high culture'.

Finally, in Poland family characteristics are the sixth factor (number of children, spouse, per capita income in the family), while in Hungary income variables (income and per capita income of the family) comprise the sixth factor.

It can therefore be concluded that in Poland the main dimensions along which industrial workers are stratified are themselves sharply separated:

1. work (connected with occupation/education);
2. background;
3. cultural activities (connected with age and spouse's educational level);
4. occupation/education (connected with the manual weighting of jobs);
5. material living conditions (connected with place of residence and holidays);
6. family situation.

In Hungary the dimensions are not so clearly separated. There is a closer connection between work and occupational-educational situation, but the fourth factor is not really one dimension of stratification but rather a variety of factors causing social deprivation in separate areas (housing situation, manual weight of work, work schedule). Here too material living conditions do not represent an independent dimension, the housing situation being connected with deprivation, and the supply of consumer durable goods with cultural activities.

Previous analysis has indicated that the multiple dimensions are more clearly separated in Poland, while the uni-dimensional socio-occupational grouping more accurately describes the stratification of industrial workers in Hungary. A separate analysis of the two countries would call for a reduced usage of the plural dimensions in Hungary and an amending of socio-occupational grouping in Poland by incorporating the other dimensions. However, an international comparison calls for unified methods, so by means of discrimination analysis[8] we examined how far socio-occupational grouping could be reconstructed with the aid of given dimensions and the variables we had employed.

The canonic correlation of the four dimensions (the variables representing them) and the socio-occupational groups were calculated together with a reproduction coefficient for the same set of variables, which shows, with the help of the discrimination function, what percentage of respondents can be categorized straightforwardly in the socio-occupational group to which they belong according to their qualification and job (see Table 3). The result is that in both countries, and particularly in Hungary, work primarily determines the internal stratification of industrial workers. If the characteristics of work are known, then the socio-occupation group of 49 percent of respondents in Hungary and 44 percent in Poland is unambiguous. The discrimination functions revealed that such groups can be delineated only if qualifications necessary for work and the weight of manual work are known.

TABLE 3
Socio-occupation Groups and the Canonic Correlation and Reproduction Coefficient between the Selected Dimensions

	Canonic correlation		Reproduction coefficient	
	Hungary	Poland	Hungary	Poland
			%	%
1. Work dimension	0.80	0.72	49	44
2. Material living conditions dimension	0.41	0.49	33	32
3. Cultural activity	0.48	0.49	39	38
4. Mobility dimension	0.23	0.35	10	11
Total of variables belonging to dimensions 1-4	0.82	0.78	56	52

A further 7 percent in Hungary and 8 percent in Poland can be assigned unambiguously to a group if the eleven variables making up the other three dimensions are known. These eleven variables include cultural activities (reading and the frequency of participation in 'high culture') and material living conditions (in Hungary the order is consumer durable goods, income and housing, and in Poland it is income, consumer durable goods and housing). Categorization of the population is improved only very slightly if background and the educational level of the spouse are taken into consideration.

The degree of congruence characterizing social stratification is indicated by the fact that variables associated with work serve to categorize 50 percent of those in the various socio-occupational groups; material living conditions and cultural activities, 33⅓ percent; and parents and spouse, 10 percent.

It is interesting to attempt to categorize workers whose socio-occupational group is itself ambiguous, and here the complete list of variables can be taken into account. Forty-four percent of respondents in Hungary and 48 percent in Poland cannot be unambiguously categorized. In both countries there is 10 percent who, using their occupational particulars as a base, can be categorized as non-manual workers, although they are in fact engaged in manual work, or vice versa. This means that 90 percent of workers can unambiguously be categorized as manual or non-manual workers if their formal occupational particulars are examined.

As a result of the narrowing of the gap between manual and non-manual workers, 20 percent of skilled workers in Hungary and 15 percent in Poland, and 24 percent of skilled workers with a dominant task in Hungary and 21 percent in Poland, are in an identical social situation to that of non-manual workers. In Hungary 17 percent of administrative workers (20 percent in Poland) are in an identical social situation to that of manual workers. With regard to other strata, there is only an insignificant number of workers whose manual or non-manual status cannot be differentiated. The convergence between manual and non-manual workers is far from being as extensive as is frequently supposed, although it does exist as far as skilled workers and administrative workers are concerned.

If we return to the original socio-occupational categories — unskilled worker, skilled worker, white-collar worker and professional — then the categorization of 72 percent of respondents in Hungary and 66 percent in Poland is unambiguous. In Hungary 18 percent and in Poland 24 percent, of manual and non-manual workers can be categorized according to objective characteristics, and 16 percent in Hungary and 14 percent in Poland can be categorized according to qualifications.

Table 4 illustrates that the social situation of unskilled workers is the most unambiguous in Hungary (70 percent) while the situation of skilled workers is the most ambiguous (38 percent).

TABLE 4
Categorization Based on Discrimination Functions Calculated from the Complete List of Variables

Original group	New categorization based on the discrimination function															
	Hungary								Poland							
	1	2	3	4	5	6	7	8	1	2	3	4	5	6	7	8
1. Unskilled workers	70	15	10	3	1	—	—	—	56	16	16	3	7	1	1	—
2. Unskilled foremen	18	59	10	7	7	—	—	—	21	55	5	2	14	4	—	—
3. Skilled workers	15	14	38	9	13	6	4	1	15	9	48	11	13	2	2	—
4. Administrative workers	7	1	6	56	3	13	9	6	—	6	10	52	4	10	17	2
5. Skilled foremen	7	16	14	4	40	14	3	3	9	20	11	8	39	6	5	2
6. Medium-level managers	1	1	1	18	8	45	11	16	2	2	3	14	9	42	12	16
7. Professionals	—	—	—	11	1	8	61	19	—	—	2	23	5	14	43	14
8. Managers	—	—	—	4	—	15	19	63	—	—	—	—	—	17	21	62

Even though extreme groups are always more unambiguous when such a method is used, the Hungarian differences between the categories exceed methodological distortion, while in Poland there are no significant differences. In Hungary the largest transition exists between subordinate and leading professionals, and the sub-categorization and the over-categorization counterbalance each other. In Poland the actual social situation tends to deteriorate according to socio-occupational group, with the exception of administrative clerical workers, 20 percent of whom live in a social situation identical to professionals. Such data support earlier conclusions that the social distance between professionals and white-collar workers is smaller in Poland, where the conventional integration prevailing among non-manual workers has survived.

If the discriminatory effect of individual dimensions is examined, further conclusions can be drawn. In Poland, in terms of the work dimension, almost 40 percent of the skilled workers are not separated from the unskilled workers with regard to work characteristics, despite minor differences in the tasks of people in various positions. In Hungary the work of leading and subordinate professionals is similar, as one-quarter of the professionals in 'medium' positions carry out similar work to subordinate professionals.

With regard to material living conditions in Hungary, the financial situation of the unskilled group, administrative workers, subordinate professionals and skilled workers is extremely differentiated. The material living conditions of almost a third of each group are similar to groups above or below them in the division of labour.

Although average material living conditions coincide with the hierarchy of socio-occupational groups, with the exception of leading professionals, there is extreme inconsistency within each group. However, this inconsistency is less in Poland, where a bigger proportion can be assigned to their own group, or to the group nearest to their own, if material living conditions are taken into account. In Poland, therefore, inequalities in living conditions more or less follow the hierarchy of the division of labour, while in Hungary such inequalities cross-cut it to quite a large extent.

In Hungary there are small differences in the cultural activities of the two non-manual categories, and also between top skilled workers and non-manual workers. In Poland, with the exception of the subordinate and middle-level professionals, there is substantial descent down the scale. This is the only dimension where administrative clerical workers are nearer to manual workers than to other non-manual workers.

From the point of view of mobility, in Hungary there is consistency only where subordinate professionals are concerned. If the educational levels of spouse and parents are taken into consideration, more than half of the respondents unambiguously belong to the professional category. The other categories are more prone to inconsistency, particularly where skilled workers in leading positions are concerned. In Poland there is a relatively high congruence between the socio-occupational categories and chances of mobility where the non-manual workers are concerned, which is another indication that the traditional integration of non-manual workers is relatively strongly reproduced.

In both countries our investigations indicated that the internal stratification of industrial workers is determined by their position in the division of labour, character of work, educational level and qualifications.

Status inconsistency is relatively high in both countries, but it is particularly high in Hungary, where living conditions especially are inconsistent with other elements of social stratification. There is also extensive incongruence between individual elements of material living conditions. The main forms of cultural activities, particularly reading habits and participation in 'high culture', are quite strongly category-specific, while the frequency of participation in popular culture is influenced primarily by demographic factors (age, family status and number of children). In Hungary holidays and recreation are more strongly category-specific.

In the Polish internal stratification of industrial workers, the traditional manual/non-manual demarcation line remains relatively strong, which means that manual and non-manual workers are less internally differentiated. In Hungary social differentiation *within* the manual and non-manual categories surpasses the average differences *between* the two categories. However, the convergence of manual and non-manual workers in Hungary is not so extensive as is often supposed either, and there is a blurring of the demarcation lines between them rather than a growing similarity in the character of work. There does however remain a substantial difference in cultural activities. Differences between manual and non-manual workers have largely disappeared in the dimension of material living conditions, but it must be taken into account that material living conditions vary greatly within each category.

In Poland the difference between the administrative clerical workers and professionals is most extensive in the field of cultural activities, while in all other respects clerical workers are closer to professionals than to skilled workers.

There are important differences between the two countries in the stratification of workers. In Poland the situation of manual workers is characterized primarily by the fact that they are, generally speaking, in a worse situation than non-manual workers. In Hungary there is a definite layer in the manual worker categories, particularly among skilled workers, which is above average on every dimension examined. The social situation of this group is identical, or at least similar to, the average social situation of the professionals. There are no significant differences between the average skilled workers and the administrative clerical workers; that is to say, what differences there are counterbalance one another. There are relatively greater differences between unskilled and skilled workers in Hungary than in Poland.

In both countries the transmission of social inequalities between generations is relatively slight, while mobility is high. At the same time, from the point of view of background and marriage, there is a particular 'openness' in the middle grades of the hierarchy, which decreases at both extremes.

To summarize, it can be said that overall there is more identity, more similarities than differences, within the internal stratification of the industrial workers of the two countries. The biggest difference is that in Poland the traditional structure of society survives to a greater extent, particularly the demarcation line between the manual and non-manual workers. This traditional difference has disappeared to some extent in Hungary, because of the social developments of the past 30-35 years.

However, differences of a new type have developed, and the accumulation of differences and inequalities are broken up more by status inconsistencies in Hungary than in Poland. In addition, there is a considerable differentiation among manual workers as a whole, since there is a big gap between the elite and the unskilled, deprived, layer of workers. In Poland the situation of the skilled workers is unfavourable because of the relative small differences between the categories. The uniformity of the workers and the differences between manual and non-manual workers therefore become more pronounced.

NOTES

1. Research carried out in socialist countries over the past 20 years — from Wesołowski to Ferge, and from Skaratan to Kjuranov — usually comes to the conclusion that, with the increase of class differences, occupational differences also increase in social differentiation.

2. With regard to the concept of status inconsistency, see Gerhard Lenski, *Power and Privilege*, New York, 1966. In socialist countries this phenomenon has been analysed in detail by Wesołowski and Slomczynski; see their Lectures delivered in Jablonna, 1974.

3. A more detailed description of individual variables is contained partly in earlier chapters, and partly in the methodological Appendix.

4. With regard to canonic correlation, see John Van der Geer, *Introduction to Multivariate Analysis for the Social Sciences*, San Francisco, 1971, Chapter 14.

5. Concerning sample construction, the main criterion of selection was job category in Hungary, and manual and non-manual category in Poland; within these categories educational level was also taken into consideration. However, this difference did have an effect. When interpreting results we were uncertain how far the differences between the two countries actually resulted from variation in differentiation and how far from differences in sampling. A methodological experiment was begun in which we tried to re-categorize the Hungarian sample according to the Polish sample. Skilled workers with a maximum of eight years of education were placed among unskilled workers, unskilled workers matriculating from school were placed with skilled workers, and managers with a high level of education were placed among clerical workers with a low level of education. The same tests were then conducted in relation to the rearranged sample, but there was hardly any change in the results. The analysis therefore shows the difference to be between the two countries and not merely to reflect the difference between the two processes of sampling. With regard to the canonic correlation calculations, these changed only to a minimal extent where work, demographic factors and material living conditions were considered. All the other values remained unchanged. In the analysis of the main component, only the connection between the socio-occupation group and the main component showed a deterioration, as the correlation between the educational level and this variant increased, but in the factor analysis exactly the same factors were extracted.

6. An excellent summary on the analysis of the main component and other forms of factor analysis can be found in the work of Mary J. Harman, *Modern Factor Analysis*, Chicago, 1967. Here the non-iterate first factor is the main component.

7. See N.H. Nie, C.H. Hull, J.G. Jankins, K. Steinbrenner and D.H. Bent: Statistical Package for the Social Sciences, 2nd ed., New York, 1975, pp. 468-514.

8. Ibid., pp. 434-67.

APPENDIX

A SHORT DESCRIPTION OF THE SURVEY

Maria Jarosińska and Ferenc Kovács

Some description of the survey seems to us to be a necessary supplement to this book, which is based on empirical data collected simultaneously in both countries (and in some other socialist countries as well). We would like therefore to devote a few words to the sampling procedures and the instruments we have used in this survey.

SAMPLING

Representation was not the basic principle of sampling. Instead, quota sampling, which represents the inter-ratio of the four groups of industrial workers (according to most recent data available at the time of the sample design) was used.
The groups are as follows:

1. unskilled and semi-skilled workers;
2. skilled manual workers;
3. white-collar workers (non-manual workers without a degree or managerial post);
4. professionals (including managers).

In Poland the following industrial branches were included: (1) energy, (2) metallurgy, (3) engineering, (4) chemical, (5) mineral (building material), (6) wood and paper, (7) lighting and (8) food. In Hungary the branches selected were: (1) metallurgy, (2) engineering, (3) building material, (4) chemical, (5) wood processing (6) paper and printing, (7) textile, (8) leather, fur and shoe, (9) clothing and (10) food.

The Polish sample was designed according to the latest statistics available at the end of 1978.[1]

It was agreed that, as a minimum, the selected sample should consist of 2,000 and that 300 people should be represented in each socio-occupational category. As group 4 (professionals) was over-represented, two samples emerged, which were separately handled in the data processing and in the analysis:

1. sample A, which was not proportionate, because of the over-representation of the professionals and was therefore used for comparative purposes;
2. sample B, which did reflect the proportions existing in the country's industry.

Such samples facilitated comparison between countries, in terms of the connections that can be revealed by regression, factor analysis and other such techniques.

The next step was to fill-up the samples from the selected industrial branches and companies. The Polish researchers selected 1,288 enterprises from a complete list of the local technological units (plants and factories) in the selected industrial branches, and described them in terms of the number of employees, the supply of assets, the character of the working conditions, the size of their locations and their regional situations. The selection of respondents was carried out by means of drawing lots, based on a table of random numbers from a list of the workers in the units. The same method was used to select the number of male and female respondents according to the four socio-occupational categories. The interviewers, about 130 people, personally chose their respondents from the files of the units.

The method of the Hungarian researchers was simpler. They did not compile a representative sample, only a sample proportionate with the quota. From the 10 selected industrial branches, one company was selected from each (3 from the largest, the engineering branch, and 2 from the next largest branch, the food industry). The total was 13 companies of different sizes, operating in towns varying in size and situated in different regions of the country. As far as possible they represented different technological levels. Sociologists of the Hungarian Sociological Association undertook the organization of the sampling and collection of information. The 9 sociologists[2] looked through the alphabetical files of the companies' labour departments, selected respondents with the prescribed characteristics, and then organized the data collection. The Hungarian sample was therefore selected from 13 companies belonging to 10 industrial branches, and the basis was the fairly reliable random alphabetical order of workers' names. The 13 companies in the 11 towns represented 7 of the country's 20 administrative units (19 plus Budapest).

TABLE 1
Division of Processed Material

	Poland			Hungary		
	A sample	B sample		A sample	B sample	
	N	*N*	%	*N*	*N*	%
1. Unskilled and semi-skilled workers	968	968	52.6	822	822	41.2
2. Skilled workers	675	501	27.5	645	645	32.2
3. White-collar workers	411	305	16.7	382	382	19.1
4. Professionals	294	56	3.2	301	150	7.5
Total	2,348	1,830	100	2,150	1,999	100

Answers given in Table 1 were processed. The questionnaires were filled in during working hours in the selected enterprises. Respondents were supplied with detailed instructions to help them apply uniform criteria, and they could obtain additional explanations from the interviewers.

In Hungary the interviews were carried out mostly at the respondents' place of work, whereas in Poland they were held in respondents' homes.

INSTRUMENTS

The interviews consisted of the following issues:

1. *Work:* (a) analysed with regard to the situation existing in a particular enterprise (e.g., working hours, organization, the position in the management structure, etc.); (b) workers' attitudes and interpersonal relations (e.g., the importance attached to various features of work, to participation in management, estimated future prospects and interpersonal relations in a small group). Information was also obtained about the choice of a worker's first job.

2. *Social activity:* (a) workers' affiliation to various organizations and their functions; workers' participation in any voluntary activity and its function. Information was obtained on workers' opinions about participation in management.

3. *Living conditions:* analysed with regard to income, possession of consumer durables and family situation.

4. *Participation in culture and leisure:* analysed with regard to reading habits, television, visits to theatres, museums, sports events, etc. and aspirations in this respect. Leisure was analysed with regard to the worker's last holiday, length of time of holiday, the manner in which it was spent, and aspirations in this connection.

5. *Intra-* and *inter-generational social mobility:* analysed with regard to the social position that respondents and respondents' parents had at the time of their first job, and with regard to their present social position and future aspirations. The respondents' close social circle (i.e. socio-economic position of his/her spouse, working children, siblings, closest friend) was studied with regard to its heterogeneity or homogeneity.

6. *Respondent's basic characteristics:* personal (age and sex) and social, i.e. level of education (including motives for continuing or discontinuing further studies); social background; permanent residence; service in the enterprise; etc. The physical and mental effort required occupationally, working conditions, level of training required, necessary and possible social contacts in an enterprise and technical equipment were investigated. Time-budgets of particular tasks (direct material production, its simple and complex servicing, etc.) were also examined.

NOTES

1. Polish sources used: Spis Kadrowy, 1973; GUS, Warsaw, 1978. Hungarian sources used: *Industrial Data* (in Hungarian), KSH, Budapest, 1978. *Manpower Data Concerning State Industrial Employees* (in Hungarian) KSH, Budapest, 1972.

2. In Miskolc and Borsodnádasd, Dr Alfred Lehoczky; in Debrecen and Berettyóujfalu, Dr József Ullaga; in Budapest, János Szeich, Mrs J. Rádai, Mrs I. Hornyák and Zoltán Zétényi; in Szeged and Hódmezovásárhely, Ilona Czabai; in Zalaegerszeg, Lajos Kovács; at Kecskémet and Kiskunmajsa, Dr J. Szöcs; and in Dunaujvárost, Zoltan Zétányi.

NOTES ON CONTRIBUTORS

Lidia Beskid is a Professor at the Institute of Philosophy and Sociology of the Polish Academy of Sciences. Her principal area of interest is consumption patterns among different social strata and the economic roots of social inequality. She is author of *Changes in Consumption in Poland* (Warsaw, 1972) and *Consumption Patterns among Workers' Families* (Warsaw, 1977).

Maria Jarosińska is Assistant Professor at the Institute of Philosophy and Sociology of the Polish Academy of Sciences. Her principal area of interest is social differentiation among workers with particular reference to working conditions. She is the author of *Adjustment of Young Workers to the First Job* (Warsaw, 1972).

Tamás Kolosi is head of the department of social stratification studies at the Institute of Social Sciences, Budapest. He is the author of many social science publications.

Ferenc Kovács is a researcher at the Institute of Social Sciences, Budapest. His book *On the Political and Ideological Education and Activity of the Working Class* was published in Budapest in 1976.

Edmund Wnuk-Lipiński is Associate Professor of Sociology at the Institute of Philosophy and Sociology of the Polish Academy of Sciences. He is the author of several books and articles on social policy and inequality in Eastern Europe with particular focus on cultural activities and the use of leisure.

Volumes in the SAGE Studies in International Sociology Book Series

CRISIS AND CONTENTION IN SOCIOLOGY *Editor* Tom Bottomore 1975
THE MILITARY AND THE PROBLEM OF LEGITIMACY *Editors* Gwyn Harries-Jenkins and Jacques van Doorn 1976
SOCIOLOGICAL PRAXIS: Current Roles and Settings *Editors* Elisabeth Crawford and Stein Rokkan 1976
INTERNAL MIGRATION: The New World and the Third World *Editors* Anthony H Richmond and Daniel Kubat 1976
THE INTELLIGENTSIA AND THE INTELLECTUALS: Theory, Method and Case Study *Editor* Aleksander Gella 1976
POWER AND CONTROL: Social Structures and Their Transformation *Editors* Tom R Burns and Walter Buckley
BEYOND THE NUCLEAR FAMILY MODEL: Cross-Cultural Perspectives *Editors* Tom R Burns and Walter Buckley
SCIENTIFIC-TECHNOLOGICAL REVOLUTION: Social Aspects R Dahrendorf et al 1977
POWER, PARADIGMS, AND COMMUNITY RESEARCH *Editors* Roland J Liebert and Allen W Imershein 1977
WORK AND TECHNOLOGY *Editors* Marie R Haug and Jacques Dofny 1977
EDUCATION IN A CHANGING SOCIETY *Editors* Antonina Kloskowska and Guido Martinotti 1977
ORGANIZATION AND ENVIRONMENT: Theory, Issues and Reality *Editor* Lucien Karpik 1978
DISASTERS: Theory and Research *Editor* E L Quarantelli 1978
SEX ROLES AND SOCIAL POLICY: A Complex Social Science Equation *Editors* Jean Lipman-Blumen and Jessie Bernard 1979
THE SOCIAL ECOLOGY OF CHANGE: From Equilibrium to Development *Editors* Zdravko Mlinar and Henry Teune 1979
IDENTITY AND RELIGION: International, Cross-Cultural Approaches *Editor* Hans Mol 1979
LEGITIMATION OF REGIMES: International Frameworks for Analysis *Editor* Bogdan Denitch 1979
WORK AND POWER: The Liberation of Work and the Control of Political Power *Editors* Tom R Burns, Lars Erik Karlsson & Veljko Rus 1980
NATIONAL AND ETHNIC MOVEMENTS *Editors* Jacques Dofny and Akinsola Akiwowo 1980
THE QUALITY OF LIFE: Comparative Studies *Editors* Alexander Szalai and Frank M Andrews 1980
FACTOR ANALYSIS AND MEASUREMENT IN SOCIOLOGICAL RESEARCH: A Multi-Dimensional Perspective *Editors* David J Jackson and Edgar F Borgatta 1980
MASS MEDIA AND SOCIAL CHANGE *Editors* Elihu Katz and Tamás Szecskö 1981
BIOGRAPHY AND SOCIETY: The Life History Approach in the Social Sciences *Editor* Daniel Bertaux 1981
SPONTANEITY AND PLANNING IN SOCIAL DEVELOPMENT *Editor* Ulf Himmelstrand 1981
CROSS NATIONAL REHABILITATION POLICIES: A Sociological Perspective *Editor* Gary L Albrecht 1981
THE NEW INTERNATIONAL ECONOMY *Editors* Harry Makler, Alberto Martinelli, and Neil Smelser 1982
THE SOCIOLOGY OF EDUCATIONAL EXPANSION: Take-off, Growth and Inflation in Educational Systems *Editor* Margaret S Archer 1982
OLD AGE AND THE WELFARE STATE *Editor* Anne-Marie Guillemard 1983